Gertrude Lowthian Bell

Safar Nameh

Persian Pictures

Gertrude Lowthian Bell

Safar Nameh
Persian Pictures

ISBN/EAN: 9783337294748

Printed in Europe, USA, Canada, Australia, Japan

Cover: Foto ©Thomas Meinert / pixelio.de

More available books at **www.hansebooks.com**

SAFAR NAMEH

PERSIAN PICTURES

A BOOK OF TRAVEL

LONDON
RICHARD BENTLEY AND SON
Publishers in Ordinary to Her Majesty the Queen
1894
[*All rights reserved*]

CONTENTS

	PAGE
AN EASTERN CITY	1
THE TOWER OF SILENCE	19
IN PRAISE OF GARDENS	28
THE KING OF MERCHANTS	42
THE IMAM HUSSEIN	51
THE SHADOW OF DEATH	67
DWELLERS IN TENTS	83
THREE NOBLE LADIES	96
THE TREASURE OF THE KING	112
SHEIKH HASSAN	126
A PERSIAN HOST	143
A STAGE AND A HALF	156
A BRIDLE-PATH	168
TWO PALACES	187
THE MONTH OF FASTING	205
REQUIESCANT IN PACE	219
THE CITY OF KING PRUSIAS	236
SHOPS AND SHOPKEEPERS	247
A MURRAY OF THE FIRST CENTURY	260
TRAVELLING COMPANIONS	275

ERRATUM.

Page 138, line 2, *for* 'bouches de cheveux' *read* 'bouches de chevaux.'

'PERSIAN PICTURES.'

PERSIAN PICTURES

AN EASTERN CITY

THE modern capital of Persia lies in a plain ringed half-way round by mountains, which on the northern side touch with frozen summits the regions of eternal snow, and on the east sink into low ranges of hills, stretching their naked arms into the desert. It is the chief city of a land of dust and stones—waste and desolate, Persia unfolds her monotonous length, broken only by ridges of hills even more barren than the plain itself, southward from the gates of Tehran. There is a certain fine simplicity in a landscape from which the element of water, with all the varied life it brings in its murmuring train, is entirely absent. The empty world looks like a great room cleared for the reception of some splendid company; presently it will be filled by a vast pageant of men or angels: their lance-heads will flash back the dazzling rays of the sun, their banners will float out many-coloured against the sombre background, the peal of their trumpets will re-echo from mountain to mountain. But no! day after day rises upon the same silence, the same solitude, and at length the watcher turns away impatiently, with the conviction that he has been gazing with futile expectation upon the changeless features of the dead. The pageant has long since swept over the land—swept onward. Mother of human energies, strewn with the ruins of a Titanic past, Persia has slipped out of the vivid world, and the simplicity of her landscape is the fine simplicity of death. 'Alas, poor Yorick!' says Hamlet, yielding, in an exceptionally unpremeditated moment, the natural tribute of pity from the living to the dead. Persia in such an aspect may be pitiful enough, but it is not admirable.

To the north of Tehran, however, the lower slopes of the Shimran range are clothed with gardens and cornfields, as though the dense vegetation which, by a strange freak of nature, stretches its belt of green along the southern shore of the Caspian, between the shifting sands of the Oxus and the black, naphtha-saturated earth of Baku, had sent its roots through the very heart of the mountains and found a foothold for its irrepressible luxuriance even among dust and stones. The capital itself, as you approach it from the west, presents the appearance of a wood rather than of a city—

nor minaret, nor tower, nor dome forms a landmark above it, the trees of its gardens conceal its stunted buildings, and it is not until the traveller finds himself under its very walls that he can say, 'Here is Tehran!' It owes its life to the snow mountains, from whence its water flows; the ground between them and the town is undermined by a network of passages, vaulted over with stone, and ventilated by air-holes at intervals of about fifty yards, each hole being protected by a mound of earth. Within, these arteries of the city are the width of a man's shoulders, and scarcely high enough to allow him to walk upright; he stumbles, knee-deep in water, along the uneven bed, bending himself double where the vault drops lower, squeezing past narrow corners cut out of the solid rock. On either side black apertures open into more passages, bringing in tributary streams from right and leftward, and at intervals the darkness is broken by the ray of sunlight which strikes through one of the air-holes, burying itself, like an ill-directed spear, deep into the earth. No other form of irrigation remains, no storage of water, in a country where these arts were probably familiar to the far larger population which dwelt in former ages at the foot of the mountains. The present system is clumsy and laborious. Constant watchfulness is needed to keep the Kanats from falling into disrepair and from becoming blocked by masses of roots, and if this were to be relaxed, Tehran would in a few years cease to exist.

To what merit it owes its position of capital remains a mystery. It is the seat of no native industry; arid deserts and narrow mountain-passes, traversed only by caravans of mules, cut it off from all convenient intercourse with the west. Isfahan is invested with the traditions of a former importance; about Shiraz linger the vestiges of a still mightier antiquity; Casvin lies a hundred miles nearer to the Caspian; Tehran is only a modern seat of government called to importance by the arbitrary will of the present race of sovereigns.

Many gates lead into the city, breaking the level of the mud walls, with their arches and turrets, which are decorated with tiles of faience set into patterns and pictures and inscriptions. The space enclosed by the walls is a large one, but it is not by any means filled with houses. Passing through one of the western gateways, you will find yourself at first in desolate tracts of sand, stretching between unfinished or ruined buildings; occasionally the open doorway in a long mud wall will reveal to you a luxuriant garden full of tanks and fountains and flower-beds, under whose plane-trees stands the house of some rich man who can afford himself a weekly sufficiency of water to turn the wilderness into fertile pleasure-grounds; further on you will come upon wide streets, very empty and silent, fringed by low, mud-built houses; gradually the streets narrow, the sloping counters of shops present their wares to the passers-by: fruit and vegetables, and the broad thin flaps of Persian bread; here and there a European shop-window, behind which the goods are more miscellaneous than tempting; here and there the frontage of some Government building, with a doorway gaily patterned in coloured bricks. As the streets grow narrower, they become more crowded. A kaleidoscopic world of unfamiliar figures passes to and fro beneath the white mulberry-trees which spring out between the cobble stones of the pavement: grave elders holding their cloaks discreetly round them, dervishes with a loincloth about their waists, and a brilliant scarf bound over their ragged locks, women enveloped from head to foot in loose black garments, a linen veil hanging over their faces, and making them look like the members of some strange religious order, negro slaves and white-robed Arabs, beggars and loiterers, and troops of children pressing in and out between the horsemen and the carriages. Sometimes a beggar will accost you—a woman, perhaps, drawing aside a corner of her veil and imploring alms in a sweet high voice. If you turn a deaf ear to her prayers, she will invoke curses on your head, but a copper coin will purchase you every blessing known to man, including the disappearance of the lady in question, who would otherwise have followed you with unblushing persistence, shouting, 'Pul! pul! pul!'—Money! money! money!—in your ear.

At a street corner a group of soldiers are

shaking the branches of a mulberry-tree, and eagerly devouring the sickly fruit which falls into the dust at their feet. Judging from the appearance of the Persian army, a foreigner would be tempted to conclude that it subsisted entirely upon white mulberrries, and was reduced to a state of starvation when the summer was over. The hands of paymasters are adhesive in the East: but a small proportion of his earnings reaches the common soldier, and mulberries, flavoured with dust, have at least the merit of furnishing him with an inexpensive meal. His outward man is not calculated to inspire much alarm in the breast of his enemies. His gait is slouching, his uniform torn and discoloured; not infrequently he wears his shirt outside his trousers, and the ragged flounce of brownish-gray linen hanging below his tunic lends him an air anything but martial. His temperament seems to be childlike and peaceable in the extreme. He amuses himself while he is on guard with foolish games, constructing, for instance, a water-mill of tiny wheels, which the stream in front of the palace will set a-turning, and whose movement will delight his eyes as he passes up and down. It is even related (and the tale is scarcely past credence) that on a certain occasion when a person of importance was visiting a southern fortress, he found one of the men who guarded the gateway engaged in knitting stockings, and the other turning an honest penny by the sale of apples. Nevertheless, the Shah is proud of his army. He spends happy hours devising new uniforms for his men—uniforms which are the strangest jumble of European reminiscences and an Oriental love of bright colour.

Bearing towards the north-eastern quarter of the city, you will enter a broad square which is looked upon as the ne plus ultra of municipal magnificence. It is here that the Shah causes his part in the annual Feast of Sacrifice to be performed, and here the inhabitants of Tehran assemble in great numbers to witness the slaughter of a camel by the mollahs, in token that his Majesty has not forgotten, amid the cares of State, how Abraham bound Ishmael upon the altar (for the Mohammedans assert that it was the son of Hagar who was the hero of the legend) in obedience to the command of God. Immediately after the camel has fallen he is cut up by the knives of the mollahs, and the nearest bystanders, pouncing upon some portion of the victim, make off with it at full speed to the palace, where the first comer receives a large reward.

It must be confessed that, in spite of its size, the square makes no favourable impression upon the mind of the sophisticated European. The gates leading into it are adorned with ugly modern tiles, the buildings round it lack all trace of architectural merit. Their stucco face is questionably embellished by a fresco of lions, exceedingly ill drawn, each animal looking nervously round at the sun disc with its spiked circle of rays, which rises from behind its shoulders. Nor does it contain any press of human activity to atone for its lack of beauty. About the gate which leads into the Ark, where the palace is situated, there are indeed some signs of life—groups of soldiers are diversified by the figures of servants of the palace, clad in brilliant scarlet uniforms, and mounted on horses wearing bits and collars of solid silver, and by the fantastic liveries of the Shah's runners, whose dress closely resembles that which is depicted on a court-card, and whose headgear partakes equally of the nature of a beadle's and of a jester's; but for the rest this square is comparatively empty, and the wind sweeps the dust-clouds round the park of antiquated cannon which stands in its midst.

More narrow, squalid streets bring you to the bazaar, where, though little really beautiful or precious is to be found, the thronging Oriental life is in itself an endless source of delight. Ride through it on a summer morning, when its vaulted coolness will offer you a grateful shelter from the sun, and before its activity has been hushed by the heat of mid-day. In the shadow of the entrance there stands a small merchant, posted on the doorstep like an emblem of Oriental commerce—a solemn, long-robed child, so little that his mother's heart must have ached when she trusted the dear turbaned head out of her sight. This morsel of humanity has brought some bunches of flowers to sell, and has spread them out on a large stone in front of him. In his improvised shop he stands, motionless and imperturbable, watching the comers and goers, and waiting in dignified patience till one of them shall pause and buy. Wish him good luck under your breath (for he would resent the blessings of unbelievers), and pass on beneath the dark arches of the bazaar.

Here, at any rate, is bustle enough; trains of laden mules and donkeys shoulder your horse into the gutter, paying small heed to your cries of 'Avardah!'—Make room!—skilful housewives block the narrow way, driving hard bargains under the protection of their veils; groups of hungry men cluster round the roasters of kabobs, anxiously awaiting a breakfast. The shop-keepers alone are unmoved by the universal haste, but sit cross-legged among their wares, smoking the morning kalyan. On either side of the street arched doorways lead into caravanseries and high market-places.

In one of them the sellers of cotton goods have established themselves, their counters laden with piles of cheap printed stuffs, bearing the Manchester stamp in one corner; next door is the booksellers' court, and a certain air of scholastic leisure pervades it; here are a row of fruit-shops, where the blue earthenware bowls of curds stand among heaped-up grapes and melons; there you may buy narrow-necked bottles of rose-water; further on you find yourself in a street of metal-workers, where the bright mule-bells hang in festoons over the counters; round the next corner the fires of smithies gleam on half-naked figures, labouring with strained muscles at their anvils. The whole bazaar resounds with talk, with the cries of the mule-drivers, the tinkling bells of the caravans, and the blows of the smiths' hammers. The air is permeated with the curious smell, half musty, half aromatic, of fruits and frying meats, merchandise and crowded humanity. The light comes from the top through a round hole in each of the countless tiny domes of the roof; through each hole falls a shaft of brilliant sunshine, cutting the surrounding darkness like a sword, and striking the hurrying multitude in successive flashes, white turban and bright-coloured robe gleaming—fading, gleaming—fading, in an endless sequence of sun and shadow, as their wearers pass to and fro.

So you may ride through street after narrow crooked street till your ears are full of sound, and your eyes of colour, and your mind of restless life, and before you have had time to recover your composure, you will find yourself in the sunny square, filled with stacks of hay, and tenanted by disbanded armies of mules, which lies within the Meshed Gate. Here, too, the town is afoot. Like a swarm of bees the people jostle one another through the archway. Peasants are driving in their donkeys laden with roped bundles of grass from the meadows of Shah Abdul Azim, strings of camels file through the gate, bringing in the produce of the great cities of the south and east, busy officials are hurrying Tehranwards in the early morning about their affairs, sellers of salted nuts have established themselves under the trees, beggars are lying by the roadside, pilgrims returning from Meshed hasten their step as the homeward goal comes into sight.

With the impression of the deserted western roads still fresh in your memory, the appearance of the bazaars and of this eastern gate will fill you with surprise. Tehran, which from the west looked almost like a city of the dead, cut off from intercourse with the outer world, is alive after all and in eager relationship with a world of its own. Here in the dust and the sunshine is an epitome of the living East, and standing unnoticed in such a doorway, you will admit that you have not travelled in vain. But as the wonderful procession of people files past you, too intent upon their own affairs to give you more than a contemptuous glance, you will realize what a gulf lies between you. The East looks to itself; it knows nothing of the greater world, of which you are a citizen, asks nothing of you and of your civilization.

THE TOWER OF SILENCE

HUNDREDS of years ago, when the Persian race first issued from unknown Bactria and the grim Hyrcanian forests, passing through the Caspian Gates, they came upon a fertile land lying to the north-east of the country, which was subsequently named Media. There on the edge of the province known to-day as Khorasan they founded a city, which with the rolling centuries gathered greatness and riches and power; the Greeks (for her fame had penetrated to the limits of the civilized world) called her Rages. Key to Hyrcania and Parthia, the geographical position of the Median city lent her considerable importance. The Jews knew her well: in Rages dwelt that Gabelus to whom the pious Tobit entrusted his ten talents of silver in the days of the Captivity; there Tobias was journeying when the angel Raphael met him and instructed him in the healing properties of fishes; there, relates the author of the Book of Judith, reigned Phraortes whom Nebuchadnezzar smote through with his darts and utterly destroyed.

Rages, the Ancient of Days, passed through many vicissitudes of fortune in the course of her long-drawn life. Under her walls fled the last Darius when Alexander's army chased him, vanquished at Arbela, over the wide plains of Khorasan—fled to the mountains of the Caspian to seek a luckless fate at the hands of the cruel Bactrian satrap. At Rages, perhaps, the generous Alexander mourned the untimely death of his rival, from her palaces hurled his vengeance against

Bessus, and saw the satrap dragged a captive to execution. Twice the city was destroyed, by earthquake and by Parthian invaders, twice to rise up afresh under new names. At length, in the twelfth century, an enemy more devastating than the Parthian hordes, more vindictive than the earthquake, swept over pleasant Khorasan and turned the fertile province into the wilderness it is to this day. Tartars from the uttermost ends of the earth left no stone of Rages standing, and the great Median city vanished from the history of men. A few miles to the north-east Tehran has sprung up to be the capital of modern Persia—a Persia to whom the glorious traditions of the past are as forgotten as the strength of Phraortes' walls. 'The Lion and the Lizard keep the courts where Jemshyd gloried and drank deep,' but the foundations of Rages, the mother of Persian cities, can be traced only by conjecture.

Through waste and solitary places we rode one morning to the city and the citadel of the dead. It was still so early that the sun had not overtopped the range of eastern mountains. We rode out of sleeping Tehran, and took our way along the deserted track that skirts its walls; to our left lay the wilderness, wrapped in transparent shadow, and sloping gradually upwards to the barren foot-hills over which winds the road to Meshed. Before we had gone far, with a flash and a sudden glitter, the sun leapt up above the snow-peaks, and day rushed across the plain—day, crude and garish, revealing not the bounteous plenty of the cornfields and pastures which encircled Rages, but dust and stones and desert scrub, and the naked, forbidding mountains, wrinkled by many winters.

To us, with the headlong flight of Darius and the triumph of the conqueror surging before our eyes, the broken ground round the site of the ancient stronghold piled itself into ruined turret and rampart, sank into half-obliterated fosse and ditch. Where we imagined the walls to have been, we discovered a solid piece of masonry, and our minds reeled at the thought that it was wildly possible Alexander's eyes might have rested on this even brickwork. Time has made gates in the battlements, but the desert has not even yet established unquestioned rule within them. At the foot of the wall we came upon a living pool lying under the shadow of a plane-tree. Round such a pool the sick men of Bethsaida gathered and waited for the stirring of the waters, but in Rages all was solitude, 'and the desired angel came no more.'

Towards the east two parallel lines of hills rear themselves out of the desert, dividing it from the wider stretch of desert that reaches southward to Isfahan. Between the hills lies a stony valley, up which we turned our steps, and which led us to the heart of desolation and the end of all things. Half-way up the hillside stands a tower, whose whitewashed wall is a landmark to all the country round. Even from the far distant peaks of the opposite mountains, the Tower of Silence is visible, a mocking gleam reminding the living of the vanity of their eager days. For the tower is the first stage in the weary journey of the dead; here they come to throw off the mantle of the flesh before their bones may rest in the earth without fear of defiling the holy element, before their souls, passing through the seven gates of the planets, may reach the sacred fire of the sun.

The tower is roofless; within, ten or twelve feet below the upper surface of its wall, is a chalky platform on which the dead bodies lie till sun and vultures have devoured them. This grim turret-room was untenanted. Zoroaster's religion has faded from that Media where once it reigned, and few and humble now are the worshippers who raise prayers to Ormuzd under the open heaven, and whose bodies are borne up the stony valley and cast into the Tower of Silence.

We dismounted from our horses and sat down on the hillside. The plain stretched below us like a monotonous ocean which had billowed up against the mountain flanks and had been fixed there for ever; we could see the feet of the mountains themselves planted firmly in the waves of dust, and their glistening peaks towering into the cloudless sky; the very bones of the naked earth were exposed before us, and the fashion of its making was revealed.

With the silence of an extinct world still heavy upon us, we made our way to the upper end of the valley, but at the gates of the plain Life came surging to meet us. A wild hollyhock stood sentinel among the stones; it had spread some of its yellow petals for banner, and on its uplifted spears the buds were fat and creamy with coming bloom. Rain had fallen in the night, and had called the wilderness itself to life, clothing its thorns with a purple garment of tiny flowers; the delicious sun struck upon our shoulders; a joyful little wind blew the damp, sweet smell of the reviving earth in gusts towards us; our horses sniffed the air and, catching the infection of the moment, tugged at the bit and set off at racing speed across the rain-softened ground. And we, too, passed out of the silence and remembered that we lived. Life seized us and inspired us with a mad sense of revelry. The humming wind and the teeming earth shouted 'Life! life!' as we rode. Life! life! the bountiful, the magnificent! Age was far from us—death far; we had left him enthroned in his barren mountains, with ghostly cities and out-worn faiths to bear him company. For us the wide plain and the limitless world, for us the beauty and the freshness of the morning, for us youth and the joy of living!

IN PRAISE OF GARDENS

THERE is a couplet in an Elizabethan book of airs which might serve as a motto for Eastern life: 'Thy love is not thy love,' says the author of the songs in the 'Muses' Garden of Delights' (and the pretty stilted title suits the somewhat antiquated ring of the lines):

> 'Thy love is not thy love if not thine own,
> And so it is not, if it once be known.'

If it once be known! Ah yes! the whole charm of possession vanishes before the gaze of curious eyes, and for them, too, charm is driven away by familiarity. It takes the mystery of a Sphinx to keep the world gazing for thirty centuries. The East is full of secrets—no one understands their value better than the Oriental ; and because she is full of secrets she is full of entrancing surprises. Many fine things there are upon the surface : brilliance of colour, splendour of light, solemn loneliness, clamorous activity ; these are only the patterns upon the curtain which floats for ever before the recesses of Eastern life, its essential charm is of more subtle quality. As it listeth, it comes and goes ; it flashes upon you through the open doorway of some blank, windowless house you pass in the street, from under the lifted veil of the beggar woman who lays her hand on your bridle, from the dark, contemptuous eyes of a child ; then the East sweeps aside her curtains, flashes a facet of her jewels into your dazzled eyes, and disappears again with a mocking little laugh at your bewilderment ; then for a moment it seems to you that you are looking her in the face, but while you are wondering whether she be angel or devil, she is gone.

She will not stay—she prefers the unexpected; she will keep her secrets and her tantalizing charm with them, and when you think you have caught at last some of her illusive grace, she will send you back to shrouded figures and blank house-fronts.

You must be content to wait, and perhaps some day, when you find her walking in her gardens in the cool of the evening, she will take a whim to stop and speak to you, and you will go away fascinated by her courteous words and her exquisite hospitality.

For it is in her gardens that she is most herself—they share her charm, they are as unexpected as she. Conceive on every side such a landscape as the dead world will exhibit when it whirls naked and deserted through the starry interspace—a gray and featureless plain, over which the dust-clouds rise and fall, build themselves into mighty columns, and sink back again among the stones at the bidding of hot and fitful winds ; prickly low-growing plants for all vegetation, leafless, with a foliage of thorns ; white patches of salt, on which the sunlight glitters ; a fringe of barren mountains on the horizon. . . . Yet in this desolation lurks the mocking beauty of the East. A little water and the desert breaks into flower, bowers of cool shade spring up in the midst of dust and glare, radiant stretches of soft colour gleam in that gray expanse. Your heart leaps as you pass through the gateway in the mud wall; so sharp is the contrast, that you may stand with one foot in an arid wilderness and the other in a shadowy, flowery paradise. Under the broad thick leaves of the plane-trees tiny streams murmur, fountains splash with a sweet fresh sound, white-rose bushes drop their fragrant petals into tanks, lying deep and still like patches of concentrated shadow. The indescribable charm of a Persian garden is keenly present to the Persians themselves—the 'strip of herbage strown, which just divides the desert from the sown,' an endlessly beautiful parable. Their poets sing the praise of gardens in exquisite verses, and call their books by their names. I fear the Muses have wandered more often in Sa'di's Garden of Roses than in the somewhat pretentious pleasure-ground which our Elizabethan writer prepared for them.

The desert about Tehran is renowned for the beauty of its gardens. The Shah possesses several, others belong to his sons, others to powerful ministers and wealthy merchants. Sometimes across the gateways a chain is drawn, denoting that the garden is Bast—sanctuary—and into these the

European may not go; but places of refuge for the hunted criminal are, fortunately, few, and generally the garden is open to all comers.

Perhaps the most beautiful of all is one which belongs to the Shah, and which lies under a rocky hillock crowned with the walls and towers of a palace. We found ourselves at its gate one evening, after an aimless canter across the desert, and determined to enter. The loiterers in the gateway let us pass through unchallenged. We crossed the little entrance-court and came into a long dark avenue, fountains down the middle of it, and flower-beds, in which the plants were pale and meagre for want of light; roses, the pink flowers which scent the rosewater, and briars, a froth of white and yellow bloom, growing along its edges in spite of the deep shade of the plane-trees. Every tiny rill of water was fringed with violet leaves—you can imagine how in the spring the scent of the violets greets you out in the desert when you are still far away, like a hospitable friend coming open-armed down his steps to welcome you. We wandered along intersecting avenues, until we came to one broader than the rest, at the end of which stood a little house. Tiny streams flowed round and about it, flowed under its walls and into its rooms; fountains splashed ceaselessly in front of it, a soft light wind swayed the heavy folds of the patterned curtains hanging half-way down across its deep balconies. The little dwelling looked like a fairy palace, jewelled with coloured tiles, unreal and fantastic, built half out of the ripple of water, and half out of the shadowy floating of its great curtains. Two or three steps and a narrow passage, and we were in the central room—such a room to lie and dream in through the hot summer days!—

tiled with blue, in the middle an overflowing fountain, windows on either side opening down to the ground, the vaulted ceiling and the alcoved walls set with a mosaic of looking-glass, in whose diamonds and crescents the blue of the tiles and the spray of the tossing waters were reflected.

As we sat on the deep step of the window-sill, a door opened softly, and a long-robed Persian entered. He carried in his hand a twanging stringed instrument, with which he established himself at the further side of the fountain, and began to play weird, tuneless melodies on its feeble strings—an endless, wailing minor. Evening fell, and the dusk gathered in the glittering room, the fountain bubbled lower and sank into silence, the wind blew the sweet smell of roses in to us where we sat—and still the Persian played, while in the garden the nightingales called to one another with soft thrilling notes.

A week or two later we came back to Doshan Tepe. This time we found it peopled by a party of Persians. They were sitting round the edge of one of the tanks at the end of the avenue, men and little children, and in their green and yellow robes they looked to us as we entered like a patch of brilliant water-plants, whose vivid colours were not to be dimmed by the shade of the plane leaves. But the musician did not reappear; he was too wise a magician to weave his spells 'save to the span of heaven and few ears.'

There was a deserted garden at the foot of the mountains which had a curious history. It belonged to the Zil es Sultan, the Shah's eldest son, who had inherited it from his mother, that Schöne Müllerin whose beauty captivated the King of Kings in the days of his youth. The Zil (his title, being interpreted, signifies 'The shadow of the King') has fallen into disgrace. The Shah casts his shadow far, and in order that it may never grow less, the Zil is not allowed to move from Isfahan; his Shimran garden therefore is empty, and his house is falling into disrepair. It stands on the edge of a rushing mountain torrent, which, we will hope, turned the mill-wheels in old days (though some men assert that the girl was not a miller's daughter, after all), and it boasts some magnificent plane-trees, under which we picnicked one evening, hanging Persian lanterns from the boughs. The night had brought tall yellow evening primroses into flower, and their delicious smell mingled with that of the jessamine, which covered the decaying walls. The light of our lanterns shone on the smooth tree trunks, between the leaves glimmered a waning moon, and behind us the mountain sides lay in sheets of light. We did not envy the Zil his palaces in Isfahan.

Once in another garden we found the owner at home. It was early in the morning; he was standing on his doorstep, judging between the differences of two people of his village, a man and a veiled woman, who had come to seek his arbitration. They were both talking loudly, she with shrill exclamations and calls upon God to witness, in her eagerness forgetting the laws of modesty, and throwing aside her thick linen veil, that she might plead with eyes and expression, as well as voice—or perhaps it was policy, for she had a beautiful face, dark-eyed and pale, round which the folds of black cloak and white linen fell like the drapery round the head of a Madonna. When our unknown host saw us, he dismissed his clamorous petitioners, and greeted us with the courtesy which is the heirloom of the Persian race. Seats were brought for us, tea and coffee served to us, a blue cotton-clothed multitude of gardeners offered us baskets of unripe plums, dishes of lettuce, and bunches of stiffly-arranged flowers. We sat and conversed, with no undue animation, here and there an occasional remark, but the intervals were rendered sociable by the bubbling of kalyans. At length we rose to go, and as we walked down the garden-paths many compliments passed between us and our host. At the gate he assured us that our slave had been honoured by our acceptance of his hospitality, and with low bows we mounted our horses and rode away.

We had not in reality trenched upon his privacy. There was, indeed, a part of his domains where even his hospitality would not have bidden us enter. Behind the house in which we were received lay the women's dwelling, a long, low, verandaed building standing round a deep tank, on whose edge solemn children carry on their dignified games, and veiled women flit backwards and forwards. Shaded by trees, somewhat desolate and uncared-for in appearance, washed up at the further end of the garden beyond the reach of flowers, the sight of the andarun and of its inhabitants knocks at the heart with a weary sense of discontent, of purposeless, vapid lives—a wailing, endless minor.

So in the wilderness, between high walls, the secret, mysterious life of the East flows on—a life into which no European can penetrate, whose standards, whose canons, are so different from his own that the whole existence they rule seems to him misty and unreal, incomprehensible, at any rate unfathomable; a life so monotonous, so unvaried from age to age, that it does not present any feature marked enough to create an impression other than that of vague picturesqueness, of dulness inexpressible, of repose which has turned to lethargy, and tranquillity carried beyond the point of virtue.

And these gardens, also with their tall trees and peaceful tanks, are subject to the unexpected vicissitudes of Eastern fortune. The minister falls into disgrace, the rich merchant is ruined by the exactions of his sovereign; the stream is turned off, the water ceases to flow into the tanks and to leap in the fountains, the trees die, the flowers wither, the walls crumble into unheeded decay, and in a few years the tiny paradise has been swept forgotten from the face of the earth, and the conquering desert spreads its dust and ashes once more over it all.

THE KING OF MERCHANTS

QUITE early in the morning we rode out to his garden. We had left Tehran, and moved up to one of the villages lying eight miles nearer the mountains on the edge of the belt of fertile country which stretches along their lower slopes. Our road that morning led us still further upwards through a green land full of wild-flowers, which seemed to us inexpressibly lovely after the bare and arid deserts about the town. The air was still fresh with the delicious freshness of the dawn; dew there was none, but a light, brisk wind, the sun's forerunner, had shaken the leaves and grass by the roadside and swept the dust from them, and dying, it had left some of its cool fragrance to linger till mid-day in shadowy places. We rode along dark winding paths, under sweet-smelling walnut-trees, between the high mud walls of gardens, splashing through the tiny precious streams which came down to water fields, where, although it was only June, the high corn was already mellowing amidst a glory of purple vetch. The world was awake—it wakes early in the East. Laden donkeys passed us on their way to the town, veiled women riding astride on gaily-caparisoned mules, white-turbaned priests, and cantering horsemen sitting loosely in their padded saddles. Ragged beggars and half-naked dervishes were encamped by the roadside, and as we passed implored alms or hurled imprecations, as their necessity or their fanaticism indicated.

At the foot of the mountains we stopped

before a long wall, less ruinous than most—
a bare mud wall, straight and uncompromising, with an arched doorway in the
midst of it. At our knock the double panels
of the door were flung open, disclosing a
flight of steps. Up these we climbed, and
stood at the top amazed by the unexpected
beauty which greeted us. The garden ran
straight up the hillside; so steep it was that
the parallel lines of paths were little but
flights of high narrow stairs—short flights
broken by terraces on which flower-beds
were laid out, gay with roses and nasturtiums
and petunias. Between the two staircases,
from the top of the hill to the bottom, ran a
slope of smooth blue tiles, over which flowed
cascades, broadening out on the terraces into
tiny tanks and fountains where the water
rose and fell all day long with a cool, refreshing sound, and a soft splashing of spray.
We toiled up the stairs till we came to the

topmost terrace, wider than the rest. Here the many-coloured carpet of flowers gave place to a noble grove of white lilies, which stood in full bloom under the hot sunlight, and the more the sun blazed the cooler and whiter shone the lilies, the sweeter and heavier grew their fragrance. Those gardens round Tehran to which we were accustomed had been so thickly planted with trees that no ray of light had reached the flower-beds, but here in the hills, where the heat was tempered by cool winds, there was light and air in abundance. On the further side of this radiant bodyguard was a pleasure-house—not a house of walls, but of windows and of shutters, which were all flung open, a house through which all the winds of heaven might pass unchallenged. There was a splashing fountain in the midst of it, and on all four sides deep recesses arched away to the wide window-frames. We entered, and flinging ourselves down on the cushions of one of these recesses, gazed out on the scene below us. First in the landscape came the glitter of the little garden; lower down the hillside the clustered walnuts and poplars which shaded the villages through which we had ridden; then the brown, vacant plain, with no atmosphere but the mist of dust, with no features but the serpentining lines of mounds which marked the underground course of a stream, bounded far away by a barren line of hills, verdureless and torrent-scored, and beyond them more brown plains, fainter lines of barren hills to the edge of the far horizon. Midway across the first desert lay a wide patch of trees sheltering the gardens of Tehran. Down there in the town how the sun blazed! The air was a haze of heat and dust, and a perspiring humanity toiled, hurrying hither and thither, under the dark arches of the bazaar; but in the garden of the King of Merchants all day long cool winds blew from the gates of the hills, all day long the refreshing water rippled and sparkled, all day long the white lilies at our feet lay like a reflection of the snow-capped mountains above us.

We sat idly gazing while we sipped our glasses of milkless tea much sugared, nibbled sweetmeats from the heaped-up dishes on the ground beside us, handed round the gurgling kalyans, and held out our hands to be filled with stalkless jessamine blossoms deliciously scented. At noon we rose, and were conducted yet deeper into the domains of the royally hospitable merchant—up more flights of steps, past a big tank at the further side of which stood the andarun, the women's lodging, where thinly-clad and shrouded forms stepped silently behind the shutters at our approach, down long shady paths till we came to another guest-house standing at the top of another series of cascades and fountains. Here an excellent repast was served to us—piles of variously flavoured rice mixed with meat and fruits and sauces, roasted kabobs, minces wrapped in vine-leaves, ices, fruits, and the fragrant wine of Shiraz.

Towards the cool of the evening the King of Merchants appeared on the threshold of his breeze-swept dwelling, a man somewhat past the prime of life, with a tall and powerful figure wrapped in the long brown cloak, opening over the coloured under-robe and spotless linen, which is the dress of rich and poor alike. He was of a pleasing countenance, straight-browed, red-lipped, with a black beard and an olive complexion, and his merry dark eyes had a somewhat unexpected twinkle under his high, white-turbaned forehead. A hospitable friend and a cheerful host is he, the ready quip, the apt story, the appreciative laugh, for ever on his lips; a man on whom the world has smiled, and who smiles back at that Persian world of his which he has made so pleasant for himself, strewing it with soft cushions and glowing carpets, and planting it round with flowers. Every evening the hot summer through, he is to be found in his airy garden at the foot of the mountains; every evening strings of guests knock at his hospitable gates, nor do they knock in vain. At the top of his many staircases he greets them, smiling, prosperous—those stairs of his need never be wearisome for alien feet to climb. He takes the new-comers by the hand, and leads them into one of his guest-houses; there, by the edge of a fountain, he spreads carpets on which they may repose themselves; there, as the night draws on, a banquet of rice and roasted meats and fruits is laid before them, tall pitchers of water, curiously flavoured sherbets, silver kalyans; and while they eat the King of Merchants sits with them and entertains them with stories garnished with many a cheerful jest, many a seasonable quotation from the poets. At length he leaves them to sleep till dawn, when they arise, and, having drunk a parting glass of weak golden tea, repair to the nearest bath, and so away from the cool mountain valley and back to the heat and labour of the day. He himself spends the night in his andarun, or lying wrapped in a blanket on the roof of his gate-house, from whence he can watch the day break over the wide plain below.

We took our share in his welcome, listened to his anecdotes, and played backgammon with him, nor did we bid him farewell until the ring of lighted lamps on the mosque close at hand warned us that unless we intended to spend the night on his house-top it was time to be gone.

THE IMAM HUSSEIN

TOWARDS the middle of July the month of Muharram began—the month of mourning for the Imam Hussein. Such heat must have weighed upon the Plain of Kerbela when the grandson of the Prophet, with his sixty or seventy followers, dug the trenches of their camp not far from the Euphrates stream. The armies of Yezid enclosed them, cutting them off from the river and from all retreat; hope of succour there was none; on all sides nothing but the pitiless vengeance of the Khalif—the light of the watch-fires flickered upon the tents of his armies, and day revealed only the barren plain of Kerbela behind them — the Plain of Sorrow and Vexation.

In memory of the sufferings and death of that forlorn band and of their sainted leader, all Persia broke into lamentation. He, the holy one, hungered and thirsted; the intercessor with God could gain no mercy from men; he saw his children fall under the spears of his enemies, and when he died his body was trampled into the dust, and his head borne in triumph to the Khalif. The pitiful story has taken hold of the imagination of half the Mohammedan world. Many centuries, bringing with them their own dole of tragedy and sorrow, have not dimmed it, nor lessened the feeling which its recital creates, partly, no doubt, because of the fresh breeze of religious controversy which has swept the dust of time perpetually from off it, but partly, too, because of its own poignant simplicity. The splendid courage which shines through it justifies its long existence. Even Hussein's enemies were moved to pity by his patient endurance, by the devotion of his followers, and by the passionate affection of the women who were with him. The recorded episodes of that terrible tenth of Muharram are full of the pure human pathos which moves and which touches generation after generation. It is not necessary to share the religious convictions of the Shiahs to take a side in the hopeless battle under the burning sun, or realize the tragic picture of the Imam sitting before his tent-door with the dead child in his arms, or lifting the tiny measure of water to lips pierced through by an arrow-shot—a draught almost as bitter as the sponge of vinegar and hyssop. 'Men travel by night,' says Hussein in the miracle play, 'and their destinies travel towards them.' It was a destiny of immortal memory that he was journeying to meet on that march by night through the wilderness, side by side with El Hurr and the Khalif's army.

Shortly after we landed in Persia we came unexpectedly upon the story of the martyrdom. In the main street of Kasvin, up which we were strolling while our horses were being changed (for we were on our way to Tehran), we found a crowd assembled under the plane-trees. We craned over the shoulders of Persian peasants, and saw in the centre of the circle a group of players, some in armour, some robed in long black garments, who were acting a passion play, of which Hussein was the hero. One was mounted on a horse which, at his entries and exits, he was obliged to force through the lines of people which were the only wings of his theatre; but except for the occasional scuffle he caused among the audience, there was little action in the piece—or, at least, in the part of it which we witnessed—for the players confined themselves to passing silently in and out, pausing for a moment in the empty space which represented the stage, while a mollah, mounted in a sort of pulpit, read aloud the incidents they were supposed to be enacting.

But with the beginning of Muharram the latent religious excitement of the East broke loose. Every evening at dusk the wailing cries of the mourners filled the stillness, rising and falling with melancholy persistence all through the night, until dawn sent sorrow-stricken believers to bed, and caused sleepless unbelievers to turn with a sigh of relief upon their pillows. At last the tenth day of Muharram came—a day of deep significance to all Mohammedans, since it witnessed the creation of Adam and Eve, of heaven and hell, of life and death; but to the Shiahs of tenfold deeper moment, for on it Hussein's martyrdom was accomplished.

Early in the afternoon sounds of mourning rose from the village. The inhabitants formed themselves into procession, and passed up the shady outlying avenues, and along the strip of desert which led back into the principal street—a wild and savage band whose grief was a strange tribute to the chivalrous hero whose bones have been resting for twelve centuries in the Plain of Kerbela. But tribute of a kind it was. Many brave men have probably suffered greater tortures than Hussein's, and borne them with as admirable a fortitude; but he stands among the few to whom that earthly immortality has been awarded which is acknowledged to be the best gift the capricious world holds in her hands. If he shared in the passionate desire to be remembered which assails every man on the threshold of forgetfulness, it was not in vain that he died pierced with a hundred spears;

and though his funeral obsequies were brief twelve hundred years ago, the sound of them has echoed down the centuries with eternal reverberation until to-day.

First in the procession came a troop of little boys, naked to the waist, leaping round a green-robed mollah, who was reciting the woes of the Imam as he moved forward in the midst of his disordered crew. The boys jumped and leapt round him, beating their breasts—there was no trace of sorrow on their faces. They might have been performing some savage dance as they came onwards, a compact mass of bobbing heads and naked shoulders—a dance in which they themselves took no kind of interest, but in which they recognised that it was the duty of a Persian boy to take his part. They were followed by men bearing the standards of the village—long poles surmounted by trophies of beads and coloured silks, streamers and curious ornaments; and in the rear came another reciter and another body of men, beating their breasts, from which the garments were torn back, striking their foreheads and repeating the name of the Imam in a monotonous chorus, interspersed with cries and groans.

But it was in the evening that the real ceremony took place. The bazaar in the centre of the village was roofed over with canvas and draped with cheap carpets and gaudy cotton hangings; a low platform was erected at one end, and the little shops were converted into what looked very like the boxes of a theatre. They were hung with bright-coloured stuffs and furnished with chairs, on which the notabilities sat and witnessed the performance, drinking sherbet and smoking kalyans the while. We arrived at about nine o'clock and found the proceedings in full swing. The tent was crowded with peasants, some standing, some sitting on the raised edge of a fountain in the centre. Round this fountain grew a mass of oleander-trees, their delicate leaves and exquisite pink flowers standing out against the coarse blue cotton of the men's clothing, and clustering round the wrinkled, toil-worn peasant faces. On the platform was a mollah, long-robed and white-turbaned, who was reading exhortations and descriptions of the martyrdom with a drawling, chanting intonation. At his feet the ground was covered with women, their black cloaks tucked neatly round them, sitting with shrouded heads and with the long strip of white linen veil hanging over their faces and down into their laps. They looked for all the world like shapeless black and white parcels set in rows across the floor. The mollah read on, detailing the sufferings of the Imam: 'He thirsted, he was an hungered!' the women rocked themselves to and fro in an agony of grief, the men beat their bare breasts, tears streamed over their cheeks, and from time to time they took up the mollah's words in weary, mournful chorus, or broke into his story with a murmured wail, which gathered strength and volume until it had reached the furthest corners of the tent: 'Hussein! Hussein! Hussein!'

It was intensely hot. Cheap European lamps flared and smoked against the canvas walls, casting an uncertain light upon the pink oleander flowers, the black-robed women, and the upturned faces of the men, streaming with sweat and tears, and all stricken and furrowed with cruel poverty and hunger — their sufferings would have made a longer catalogue than those of the Imam. The mollah tore his turban from his head and cast it upon the ground, and still he chanted on, and the people took up the throbbing cry: 'Hussein! Hussein! Hussein!'

Presently a dervish shouldered his way through the throng. A scanty garment was knotted round his loins, his ragged hair hung over his shoulders, and about his head was bound a brilliant scarf, whose stripes of scarlet and yellow fell down his naked back. He had come from far; he held a long staff in his hands, and the dust of the wilderness was on the shoes which he laid by the edge of the platform. He stood there, reciting, praying, exhorting—a wild figure, with eyes in which flashed the madness of religious fanaticism, straining forward with passionate gestures through the smoky light which shone on his brilliant headgear and on his glistening face, distorted by suffering and excitement. When he had finished speaking he stepped off the platform, picked up his shoes and staff, and hurried out into the night to bear his eloquence to other villages. . . .

There is nothing more difficult to measure than the value of visible emotion. To the Englishman tears are a serious matter; they denote only the deepest and the most ungovernable feelings, they are reserved for great occasions. Commonplace sensations are, in his opinion, scarcely worth bringing on to the surface. The facile expression of emotion in a foreigner is surprising to him — he can scarcely understand the gestures of a nation so little removed from him as the French, and he is apt to be led astray by what seems to him the visible sign of great excitement, but which to them is only a natural emphasis of speech. In the East these difficulties are ten times greater. The gesture itself has often a totally different significance; the Turk nods his head when he says 'No,' and shakes it when he wishes to imply assent; and even when this is not the case, the feeling which underlies it is probably quite incomprehensible—quite apart from the range of Western emotion—and its depth and duration are ruled by laws of which we have no knowledge. The first thing which strikes us in the Oriental is his dignified and impassive tranquillity. When we suddenly come upon the other side of him, and find him giving way, for no apparent reason, to uncontrolled excitement, we are ready to believe that only the most violent feelings could have moved him so far from his habitual calm. So it was that evening. At first it seemed to us that we were looking upon people plunged into the blackest depths of grief, but presently it dawned upon us that we were grossly exaggerating the value of their tears and groans. The Oriental spectators in the boxes were scarcely moved by an emotion which they were supposed to be sharing; they sat listening with calm faces, partook of a regular meal of sweetmeats, ices, and sherbets, and handed round kalyans with polite phrases and affable smiles. Our Persian servants were equally unmoved; they conformed so far to the general attitude as to tap their well-clad chests with inattentive fingers, but they kept the corners of their eyes fixed upon us, and no religious frenzy prevented them from supplying our every want. And on the edges of the crowd below us the people were paying no heed to what was going forward; we watched men whose faces were all wet with tears, whose breasts were red and sore with blows, stepping aside and entering into brisk conversation with their neighbours, sharing an amicable cup of tea, or bargaining for a handful of salted nuts, as though the very name of Hussein were unknown to them. Seeing this, we were tempted to swing back to the opposite extreme, and to conclude that this show of grief was a mere formality, signifying nothing—a view which was probably as erroneous as the other.

But whatever it meant, it meant something which we could not understand, and the whole ceremony excited in our minds feelings not far removed from disgust and weariness. It was forced, it was sordid, and it was ugly. The hangings of the tent looked suspiciously as though they had come from a Manchester loom, and if they had, they did not redound to the credit of Manchester taste; the lamps smelt abominably of oil, the stifling air was loaded with dust, and the grating chant of the mollahs was as tedious as the noise of machinery. How long it all lasted I do not know; we were glad enough to escape from it after about an hour, and as we walked home through the cool village street, we shook a sense of chaotic confusion from our minds, and heard with satisfaction the hoarse sounds fading gradually away into the night air. . . .

After such fashion the Shiahs mourn the death of the Imam Hussein, the Rose in the Garden of Glory; and whether he and his descendants are indeed the only rightful successors of the Prophet is a question which will never be definitely settled until the coming of the twelfth and last Imam, who, they say, has already lived on earth, and who will come again and resume the authority which his deputy, the Shah, holds in his name. 'When you see black ensigns' —so tradition reports Mohammed's words —'black ensigns coming out of Khorasan, then go forth and join them, for the Imam of God will be with those standards, whose name is El Mahdi. He will fill the world with equity and justice.'

THE SHADOW OF DEATH

SLOWLY, slowly through the early summer the cholera crept nearer. Out of the far East came rumours of death . . . the cholera was raging in Samarkand . . . it had crossed the Persian frontier . . . it is in Meshed! said the telegrams. A perfunctory quarantine was established between Tehran and the infected district, and the streams of pilgrims that flock ceaselessly to Meshed were forbidden to enter the holy city. Then came the daily bulletins of death, the number of the victims increasing with terrible rapidity. Meshed was almost deserted, for all whom the plague had spared had fled to the mountains, and when a week or two later its violence began to abate, flashed the ominous news: 'It is spreading among the villages to the westward.' From day to day it drew ever closer, leaping the quarantine bulwark, hurrying over a strip of desert, showing its sudden face in a distant village, sweeping northwards, and causing sanguine men to shake their heads and murmur: 'Tehran will be spared; it never comes to Tehran'—in a moment seizing upon the road to the Caspian, and ringing the city round like a cunning strategist. Then men held their breath and waited, and almost wished that the suspense were over and the ineluctable day were come. Yet with the cholera knocking at their doors they made no preparations for defence, they organized no hospitals, they planned no system of relief; cartloads of over-ripe fruit were still permitted to be brought daily into the town, and the air was still poisoned by the refuse which was left to rot in the streets. It was the month of Muharram; every evening the people fell into mad transports of religious excitement, crowding together in the Shah's theatre to witness the holy plays and to mourn with tears the death of Hussein. Perhaps a deeper fervour was thrown into the long prayers and a greater intensity into the wailing lamentations, for at the door the grim shadow was standing, and which of the mourners could answer for it that not on his own shoulder the clutching hand would fall as he passed out into the night? The cloud of dust that hung for ever over the desert and the city assumed a more baleful aspect; it hung now like an omen of the deeper cloud which was settling down upon Tehran. And still above it the sun shone pitilessly, and under the whole blue heaven there was no refuge from the hand of God. So the days passed, and the people drank bad water and gorged themselves on rotten fruit, and on a sudden the blow fell—the cholera was in Tehran.

Woe to them that were with child in those days and to them that were sick! One blind impulse seized alike upon rich and poor—flight! flight! All who possessed a field or two in the outlying villages, and all who could shelter themselves under a thin canvas roof in the desert, gathered together their scanty possessions, and, with the bare necessaries of life in their hands, crowded out of the northern gateways. The roads leading to the mountains were blocked by a stream of fugitives, like an endless procession of Holy Families flying before a wrath more terrible than that of Herod: the women mounted on donkeys and holding their babes in front of them wrapped in the folds of their cloaks, the men hurrying on foot by their side. For the vengeance of the Lord is swift; in the East he is still the great and terrible God of the Old Testament; his hand falls upon the just and upon the unjust, and punishes folly as severely as it punishes crime. In vain the desert was dotted over with the little white tents of the fugitives, in vain they sought refuge in the cool mountain villages. Wherever they went they bore the plague in the midst of them; they dropped dead by the roadside, they died in the sand of the wilderness, they spread the fatal infection among the country people.

Oriental fatalism, which sounds fine enough in theory, breaks down woefully in practice. It is mainly based upon the helplessness of a people to whom it has never occurred to take hold of life with vigorous hands. A wise philosophy bids men bear the inevitable evil without complaint, but we of the West are not content until we have discovered how far the coil is inevitable, and how far it may be modified by forethought and by a more complete knowledge of its antecedents. It may be that we turn the channel of immediate fate but little, but with every effort we help forward the future safety of the world. But fatalism can seldom be carried through to its logical conclusions —the attitude of mind which prevented the Persians from laying in medical stores did not save them a fortnight later from headlong flight.

The most degrading of human passions is the fear of death. It tears away the restraints and the conventions which alone make social life possible to man; it reveals the brute in him which underlies them all. In the desperate hand-to-hand struggle for life there is no element of nobility. He who is engaged upon it throws aside honour, he throws aside self-respect, he throws aside all that would make victory worth having—he asks for nothing but bare life. The impalpable danger into whose arms he may at any moment be precipitating himself unawares tells more upon his nerves and upon his imagination than a meeting with the most redoubtable enemy in the open; his courage breaks under the strain.

Such fear laid hold of the people of Tehran.

The Persian doctors, whose duty it was to distribute medicines among the sufferers, shut up their stores, and were among the first to leave the stricken city; masters turned their servants into the streets and the open fields, if they showed symptoms of the disease, and left them to die for want of timely help; women and little children were cast out of the andaruns; the living scarcely dared to bury the bodies of the dead.

One little group of Europeans preserved a bold front in the midst of the universal terror. The American missionaries left their homes in the villages and went down into the town to give what help they could to the sick, and to hearten with the sight of their own courage those whom the cholera had not yet touched. They visited the poorer quarters, they distributed medicines, they started a tiny hospital, in which they nursed those whom they found lying in the streets, giving them, if they recovered, clean and disinfected clothes, and if they died a decent burial. They tried to teach a people who received both their help and their wisdom at the point of the sword, the elementary laws of commonsense, to prevent them from eating masses of fruit, and to put a stop to a fertile cause of fresh infection by persuading them to burn the clothes of the dead instead of selling them for a few pence to the first comer.

Sometimes we would meet one of these men riding up from the town in the cool of the evening, when ceaseless labour and much watching had rendered it imperative that he should take at least one night's rest. His face had grown thin and white with the terrible strain of the work, and in his eyes was the expression which the sight of helpless suffering puts into the eyes of a brave man.

'One morning,' related the doctor months afterwards, 'as I was going out early to make my rounds, I found a woman lying on the doorstep. She was half naked, and she had been dead some hours, for her body was quite cold. A child crept round her, moaning for food, and on her breast was a little living baby fast asleep. . . . It was the most terrible thing I ever saw in my life,' he added after a moment. The missionaries were aided by one or two European volunteers and native pupils from their own schools, who stood shoulder to shoulder with them, and helped them to bear the heat and burden of the day. Their courage and their splendid endurance will remain graven on the minds of those who knew of it long after shameful memories of cowardice have been forgotten.

For it was not only the Persians who were terror-stricken; among the Europeans also there were instances of cowardice. There were men who, in spite of former protestations of indifference, turned sick and white with fear when the moment of trial came; there were those who fled hastily, leaving their servants and their companions to die in their deserted gardens; and there were those who took to their beds and who even went to the length of giving up the ghost, victims to no other malady than sheer terror. The English doctor had his hands full both in the town and in the country; by many a sick bed he brought comfort where his skill could not avail to save, and courage to many who were battling manfully with the disease.

Religious fervour grew apace under the influence of fear. Men to whom travel and intercourse with foreigners had given a semblance of Western civilization, exchanged their acquired garb for a pilgrim's cloak, and set forth on the long journey to Mecca. The air was full of rumours. It was whispered that the mollahs were working upon native fanaticism, and pointing to the presence of Europeans as a primary cause of evil which must be straightway removed. To-day an incredible number of deaths were reported to have taken place in Tehran during the last twenty-four hours, to-morrow the news would run from lip to lip that the Shah himself had succumbed. At the time when the cholera broke out in Tehran, his Majesty was making his summer journey through the country. He at once despatched an order to the effect that the disease was on no account to be permitted to come near his camp, but it was not within his conception of the duties of kingship to take precautions for the safety of any dweller in his realms but himself. He appeared to be considerably alarmed by the approach of an enemy who is no respecter of persons. He dismissed the greater part of his followers, and, making a few nights' halt in a palace in the neighbourhood of his capital, he hurried on into the mountains. Even in those nights forty or fifty people died in his camp, but he was kept in ignorance of this untoward occurrence. Fortunate indeed were those ladies of his andarun who accompanied him on his travels, or who had enough influence to succeed in having themselves transported to one of the numerous country palaces; the others were obliged to continue in the town, no one having time to spare them any attention, and it was not till the fury of the cholera was spent that the poor women were allowed to move into a less dangerous neighbourhood.

Even under the shadow of death there were incidents which were not lacking in a certain grim humour. Such, for example, was the tale of the half-mad and more than half-naked negro who lived in the desert beyond our doors, and who was accustomed to come whining to us for alms when we rode out. He must have possessed a sardonic sense of comedy, and the adventures of the Hunchback cannot have been unfamiliar to him. He had a wife lurking in the village, though we were unconscious of her existence till he came in tears to inform us of her decease, begging that he might be given money wherewith to pay for her burial. A charitable person provided him with the necessary sum, with which (having never, in all probability, seen so much silver in his dirty palm) he incontinently decamped. But before he left he took the precaution of setting up the dead body of his wife against the palings of our garden, thereby forcing the European dogs to bear twice over the expenses of her funeral. Persian beggars and cripples have more lives than they have limbs. Many good men died in Tehran, but when we returned there at the end of the season we found precisely the same group of maimed and ragged loiterers hanging about our doors.

The cholera was not of very long duration. A slight fall of rain reduced the daily number of deaths by several hundreds; before six weeks were past the people were returning to the streets they had quitted in precipitate haste; a fortnight later the surrounding villages also were free of sickness, and had resumed their accustomed aspect, except for an air of emptiness in the tiny bazaars, from which in some cases a third of the population had been reft, and a corresponding number of fresh graves in the burial-grounds. But another disease follows on the heels of cholera: typhoid fever is the inevitable result of an absolute disregard of all sanitary laws. The system of burial among the Persians is beyond expression evil. They think nothing of washing the bodies of the dead in a stream which subsequently runs through the length of the village, thereby poisoning water which is to be used for numberless household purposes, and in their selection of the graveyard they will not hesitate to choose the ground lying immediately above a kanat which is carrying water to many gardens and drinking-fountains. Even when they are buried, the bodies are not allowed to rest in peace. The richer families hold it a point of honour to lay the bones of their relations in some holy place—Kerbela, where Hussein was slain, or the sacred shrine of Meshed. They therefore commit them only temporarily to the earth, laying them in shallow graves, and covering them with an arched roof of brickwork, which practice accounts for the horrible smell round the graveyards after an outbreak of cholera. A few months later, and long before time has killed the germs of disease, these bodies are taken up, wrapped in sackcloth, and carried, slung across the backs of mules, to their distant resting-place, sowing not improbably the seeds of a fresh outbreak as they go. The wonder is, not that the cholera should prove fatal to so many, but that so large a proportion of the population should survive in a land where Ignorance is for ever preparing a smooth highway for the feet of Death.

DWELLERS IN TENTS

EVERY man, says a philosopher, is a wanderer at heart. Alas! I fear the axiom would be truer if he had confined himself to stating that every man loves to fancy himself a wanderer, for when it comes to the point there is not one in a thousand who can throw off the ties of civilized existence—the ties and the comforts of habits which have become easy to him by long use, of the life whose security is ample compensation for its monotony. Yet there are moments when the cabined spirit longs for liberty. A man stands a-tiptoe on the verge of the unknown world which lures him with its vague promises; the peaceful years behind lose all their value in his dazzled eyes; like him, 'qui n'a pas du ciel que ce qui brille par le trou du volet,' he pines to stand in the great free sunlight, the great wide world which is all too narrow for his adventurous energy. For one brief moment he shakes off the traditions of a lifetime, swept away by the mighty current which silently, darkly, goes watering the roots of his race. He, too, is a wanderer like his remote forefathers; his heart beats time with the hearts long stilled that dwelt in their bosoms, who came sweeping out of the mysterious East, pressing ever resistlessly onward till the grim waste of Atlantic waters bade them stay. He remembers the look of the boundless plain stretching before him, the nights when the dome of the sky was his ceiling, when he was awakened by the cold kisses of the wind that flies before the dawn. He cries for space to fling out his fighting arm; he burns to measure himself unfettered with the forces of God.

Many hundreds of miles away, to the southward of the Caspian Sea, lies a country still untraversed by highroad or railway line. Here rise mountains clothed in the spring with a gay mantle of crocuses and wild tulips, but on whose scorched sides the burning summer sun leaves nothing but a low growth of thorns; here are steep valleys, where the shadows fall early and rise late, strewn with rocks, crowned with fantastic crags, scarred with deep watercourses; here the hawks hover, the eagle passes with mournful cry, and the prisoned wind dashes madly through the gorge. Here lie reaches of plain bounded on all sides by the mountain wall, plateau after thorny plateau—a rolling wilderness over which the headlands stand out as over a sea. Through the middle of the plain flows a river, its stony bed cut deep into the earth; silver trout leap in its pools, strips of grass border it—stretches of pastureland in the midst of the desert—flocks of goats feed along its banks, and from some convenient hollow rises the smoke of a nomad camp.

For beautiful as it is in its majestic loneliness, this country is not one where men are tempted to seek an abiding dwelling. In the spring, when the fresh grass clothes the bottom of the valleys, in the summer, when the cool winds sweep the plain, they are content to pitch their tents here; but with the first nip of autumn cold they strike camp, and are off to warmer levels, leaving the high snow-carpeted regions empty of all inhabitants but the wild goats and the eagles. To-day, perhaps, the gloomiest depth of a narrow gorge, which looks as though from the time of its creation no living thing had disturbed its solitude, is strewn with black tents, flocks of horses and camels crop the grass by the edge of the stream, the air is full of the barking of dogs and the cries of women and children; but to-morrow no sign of life remains—the nomads have moved onward, silence has spread itself like a mantle from mountain to mountain, and who can tell what sound will next strike against their walls?

The sight fills you at first with a delightful sense of irresponsibility. Go where you will, the rocks will retain no impress of your footsteps; dwell where you please, the mountains are your only witnesses, and they gaze with equal indifference on your presence and on your absence. But the fitfulness of human habitation among them, the absence of any effort to civilize them, to make them shelter man and minister to his wants, gives them an air of stubborn hopeless sterility, very imposing, very repelling. Gradually the loneliness will strike into your heart with a feeling almost akin to horror. We are not accustomed to finding ourselves face to face with nature. Even the most trivial evidences of the lordship of man afford a certain sense of protection—the little path leading you along the easiest slope, the green bench selecting for you the best view, the wooden finger-post with 'Zum Wasserfall' written up upon it in large letters telling you what other men have thought worth seeing. Other men have been there before—they have smoothed out the way for you—you will find them waiting at the end, and ready to provide you with shelter and with food. . . . But here there is nothing—nothing but vast and pathless loneliness, silent and desolate.

For the nomads can no more give you a sense of companionship than the wild goats; they are equally unconscious of the desolation which surrounds them. All day long the men lie before the low doors of their tents lazily watching the grazing herds; towards evening, perhaps, they will stroll along the banks of the river with a bent stick for fishing-rod, dropping a skilful line into the pools where lie the guileless trout of those waters. Meantime the women sit weaving the coarse black roofs which shelter them, or twisting the yellow reeds into matting for walls, working so deftly that in an incredibly short time a new dwelling has grown under their fingers. In the clear sunlight the encampment looks sordid enough; night, which with sudden fingers sweeps away the sun, revealing the great depths of heaven and the patined stars, reveals also the mysterious picturesqueness of camp-life. The red light of the fires flickers between the tents; the crouching figures of men and women preparing the evening meal seem to be whispering incantations into the hot ashes. They rise, dim and gigantic, with faces gleaming in the uncertain starlight; they flit like demons backwards and forwards between the glowing rays of the fires and the darkness beyond. You find yourself transplanted into a circle of the Inferno, of which the shaggy dogs that leap out barking to meet you are no less vigilant guardians than Cerberus himself. A woman with neck and breast uncovered catches you by the sleeve, and offers to sell you a bowl of clotted cream or a vociferous fowl; her dark eyes glisten through the dusk as she tosses the matted hair from her forehead; perhaps if you stayed to eat at the bidding of this Queen of Dis you would be kept eternally a prisoner in her mournful domains. With the dawn the mystery vanishes—the place through which you passed last night is only a dull little camp, after all—and this woman clothed in dirty rags, is it possible that she can be the regal figure of last night?

But daylight will not bring you into closer fellowship with the nomads; even if you fall into speech with one of them, there are few common topics on which you can converse. He will question you as to your nationality. Are you a Russian? he inquires, naming probably the only European nation he knows. You try to explain that you are English, and come from far across the seas; and he listens attentively, though you know that your words throw no light on his boundless ignorance. Presently he will change the conversation to matters more within his understanding. What news is there of the Shah? Is he coming this summer to his camp at Siah Palas? Has the sickness struck him? The sickness! So with terrible significance he speaks of the cholera which is ravaging the country, and goes on to tell you that he and his family are flying before it. 'From over there they have come,' pointing to distant valleys. 'The sickness fell on them; eleven of their men died, and since they moved down here two more have been carried off.' A sudden picture of grim fear flashes up before you at his simple words. With what shapeless terror does the plague fill the feeble little camp! With what awful solemnity must the dead body invest the frail, small hut! What wailing cries take the place of all the cheerful sounds, and with what hurried dread is the corpse committed to an unremembered grave! Many processions of villages on the march pass you now, flying from the terror of death—a little herd of goats and horses driven by the children, a few camels carrying the rolled-up bundles of reed-dwellings, on the top of which sit the men of the family, women on foot following in the rear, a convoy of yellow dogs barking round the tiny caravan into whose narrow compass all the worldly goods of so many human beings are compressed.

But the nomads are not the only inhabitants of the valley; there are one or two more luxurious encampments. An Indian prince has pitched his camp there, and greets you as you pass, fishing-rod in hand, with an amicable 'Good-evenin', sar.' His scanty English, confined though it be to this one salutation, somewhat destroys the local colour of the scene. Noble Persians fly in the summer to this cool retreat, pitching elaborate tents of French or Indian manufacture by the edge of the river, stabling thirty or forty horses in the open air, riding through the country attended by an army of servants whom they carry with them even on their fishing expeditions, and who follow close behind their masters when they venture waist-high into the stream in the enthusiasm of sport. The grandees bring their women with them; white canvas walls enclose the tents of wives and daughters whom captivity holds even in these free solitudes, and their negro attendants are familiar figures by the river sallows, where their shrouded forms hover sadly. They understand camp life, these Persian noblemen; they are as much at home among the mountains as in their gardens and palaces. Their lavish magnificence is not out of keeping with the splendours of nature. . . . But you are only playing at nomads, after all, and when the moonlight strikes the wall of rock behind your camp, you try to banish from your mind the recollection of painted theatre scenes which it involuntarily suggests, and which makes it all seem so unreal to you.

Unreal—unreal! 'The fancy cannot cheat

so well as she is famed to do.' In vain you try to imagine yourself akin to these tented races, in vain you watch and imitate their comings and goings; the whole life is too strange, too far away. It is half vision and half nightmare; nor have you any place among dwellers in tents. Like the empty bottles and greased papers with which a troop of Bank-holiday Philistines sullies the purity of a purple moor, your presence is a blot on the wild surroundings, a hint of desecration.

Return to your cities, to your smooth paths and ordered lives; these are not of your kindred. The irretrievable centuries lie between, and the stream of civilization has carried you away from the eternal loneliness of the mountains.

THREE NOBLE LADIES

WHEN the Shah takes a girl into his andarun it is said to be a matter for universal rejoicing among her family, not so much because of the honour he has done her, as because her relatives look to using her influence as a means of gaining for themselves many an envied favour. For aught I know to the contrary, the girl, too, may think herself a fortunate creature, and the important position of the one man she may possibly govern may console her for the monotony of her kingdom; but however delightful as a place of abode the royal andarun may be, in one respect it must fall short of the delights of the kingdom of heaven—there cannot fail to be endless talk of marrying and giving in marriage within its walls. The number of the Shah's wives is great, and he is blessed with a proportionately large family; it must therefore be difficult to find a sufficiency of high-born suitors with whom to match his daughters. Moreover, there may be a trace of reluctance in the attitude of the suitors themselves, for the privilege of being the Shah's son-in-law is not without its disadvantages. If the nobleman selected happen to be wealthy, the Shah will make their close relationship an excuse for demanding from him large gifts; if at any subsequent period he should have a mind to take another wife, the etiquette of the Court will stand in his way; and still worse, if he be already married, he will find himself obliged to seek a divorce from his wife that he may obey the Shah's command. The negotiations preceding the match must be complicated in the extreme, and great must be the excitement in the andarun before they are concluded.

With one such household we were acquainted. The husband, whose title may be translated as the Assayer of Provinces, was a charming person, who had spent much of his youth (much also of his fortune) in Paris. He was a cultivated man and an enthusiast for sports; a lover of dogs, which for most Persians are unclean animals, and a devotee to the art of fishing. He had suffered not a little at the hands of his royal father-in-law, and had withdrawn in indignation from all public life, spending his days in hunting and shooting, in improving his breed of horses, and in looking after his estates. His residence abroad had made him more liberal-minded than most of his countrymen. He paid special attention to the education of his daughters, refused to allow them to be married before they had reached a reasonable age, and gave them such freedom as was consistent with their rank. They were two in number; we made their acquaintance, and that of the Princess their mother, one afternoon in Tehran.

Now, an afternoon call in Persia is not to be lightly regarded; it is a matter of much ceremony, and it lasts two hours. When we arrived at the house where the three ladies lived, we were conducted through a couple of courts and a long passage, and shown into a room whose windows opened into a vine-wreathed veranda. There was nothing Oriental in its aspect: a modern French carpet, with a pattern of big red roses on a white ground, covered the floor; photographs and looking-glasses hung upon the walls; the mantelpiece was adorned with elaborate vases under glass shades, and on some brackets stood plaster casts of statues. We might have imagined ourselves in a French château, but for the appearance of the châtelaine.

The Princess was a woman of middle age, very fat and very dark; her black eyebrows met together across her forehead; on her lips there was more than the suspicion of a moustache; the lower part of her face was heavy, and its outline lost itself in her neck. The indoor costume of a Persian lady is not becoming. She wears very full skirts, reaching barely to the knee, and standing out round her like those of a ballet-dancer; her legs are clothed in white cotton stockings, and on her feet are satin slippers. These details are partly concealed by an outer robe, unfastened in front, which the wearer clutches awkwardly over her bulging skirts, and which opens as she walks, revealing a length of white cotton ankles. In the case of the

Princess this garment was of pale blue brocade. She wore her hair loose, and a white muslin veil was bound low upon her forehead, falling down over the hair behind. She was too civilized a woman to have recourse to the cosmetics which are customary in the East; the orange-stain of henna was absent from her finger-nails, and in the course of conversation she expressed much disapproval of the habit of painting the eyes, and great astonishment when we informed her that such barbarism was not unknown even in England.

It must not be imagined that the conversation was of an animated nature. In spite of all our efforts and of those of the French lady who acted as interpreter, it languished woefully from time to time. Our hostess could speak some French, but she was too shy to exhibit this accomplishment, and not all the persuasions of her companion could induce her to venture upon more than an occasional word. She received our remarks with a nervous giggle, turning aside her head and burying her face in her pocket-handkerchief, while the Frenchwoman replied for her, 'Her Royal Highness thinks so and so.' When the interview had lasted for about half an hour, cups of tea were brought in and set on a round table in the midst of us; shortly afterwards the two daughters entered, sweeping over the floor towards us in green and pink satin garments, and taking their places at the table. The younger girl was about sixteen, an attractive and demure little person, whose muslin veil encircled a very round and childish face; the other was two years older, dark, like her mother, though her complexion was of a more transparent olive, and in her curly hair there were lights which were almost brown. Her lips were, perhaps, a little too thick, though they were charmingly curved, and her eyes were big and brown and almond-shaped, with long lashes and a limpid, pathetic expression—just such an expression as you see in the trustful eyes of a dog when he pushes his nose into your hand in token of friendship. Nor did her confiding air belie her: she took our hands in her little brown ones and told us shyly about her studies, her Arabic, and her music, and the French newspapers over which she puzzled her pretty head, speaking in a very low, sweet voice, casting down her black eyelashes when we questioned her, and answering in her soft guttural speech: 'Baleh Khanum'—'Yes, madam,' or with a little laugh and a slow, surprised 'Naghai-ai-r!' when she wished to negative some proposition which was out of the range of her small experience.

During the course of the next hour we were regaled on lemon ices, and after we had eaten them it was proposed that we should be taken into the garden. So we wandered out hand-in-hand, stopping to speak to an unfriendly monkey who was chained under the oleanders, and who turned a deaf ear to all our blandishments. In the garden there was a large pond, on the banks of which lay a canoe—an inconvenient vessel, one would imagine, for ladies attired in stiff and voluminous petticoats! Tents were pitched on the lawn, for our hostesses were on the eve of departure for their summer camp in the mountains, and had been examining the condition of their future lodgings. The garden, with its tents and its water, was like some fantastic opera stage, and the women, in their strange bright garments, the masqueraders, who would begin to dance a *pas de trois* before us as soon as the orchestra should strike up. But the play was unaccountably delayed, and while we sat under the trees servants appeared bringing coffee, a signal that the appointed time of our visit had come to an end, and that we might be permitted to take our leave. The girls accompanied us into the outer court, and watched us through the half-open doors till we drove away, wishing, perhaps, that they too might drive out into the world with such unfettered liberty, or perhaps wondering at our unveiled shamelessness.

We went to see the three ladies again when we were in the mountains. Their camp was pitched about a mile lower down the river than ours, on a grassy plateau, from which they had a magnificent view down the long bare valley and across mountains crowned by the white peak of Demavend. No sooner had we forded the river in front of our tents than a storm of wind and rain and hail broke upon us, but we continued dauntlessly on our way, for the day of our visit had been fixed some time before, and it was almost pleasant after the summer's drought to feel the rain beating on our faces. When we reached the Persian camp we dismounted before a canvas wall which surrounded the women's tents, a curtain was drawn aside for us by a negro slave, and we were taken into a large tent, where the Princess was sitting on a rolled-up bed for sofa. We greeted her with chattering teeth and sat down on some wooden chairs round her, carrying on a laboured conversation in the French tongue, while our wet clothes grew ever colder upon us. We remembered the steaming cups of tea of our former visit, and prayed that they might speedily make their appearance, but, alas! on this occasion they were omitted, and lemon ices alone were offered to us. It is not to be denied that lemon ices have their merit on a hot summer afternoon, but the Persian's one idea of hospitality is to give you lemon ices—lemon ices in hail storms, lemon ices when you are drenched with rain, lemon ices when a biting wind is blowing through the tent door—it was more than the best regulated constitution could stand. We politely refused them.

An important event had taken place in the household during the last two months: a marriage had been arranged between the eldest daughter and a young Persian nobleman, whose wealth and influence matched themselves satisfactorily with her rank. He, too, was spending the summer in the mountains; his camp lay a little beyond ours, and we were therefore able to observe the daily visits which took place between him and his future father-in-law, when they rode, attended by troops of mounted servants, backwards and forwards along the stony bridle-path on the opposite bank. Doubtless great discussions of the approaching marriage and of the art of fly-fishing took place in those August days. We stood in the centre of this Oriental romance, and felt as though we were lending a friendly hand to the negotiations. Certainly, if good wishes could help them, we did much for the young couple.

The Assayer of Provinces spent most of his time trout-fishing. He used to make us presents of gaudy flies manufactured by his negro slave (himself a most successful fisherman), and we found that these attracted the trout of the Lar considerably more than our March browns and palmers. The eldest daughter shared her father's taste. When she and her sister joined us in her mother's tent that thundery afternoon, we fell into a lively discussion of the joys and the disappointments of the sport, comparing the number of fish we had killed and the size of our largest victim. The Persian girls had never gone far afield—they contented themselves with the pools and streams near their tents—but that they should fish at all spoke volumes for their energy. To throw a well-considered fly is a difficult art at best, but to throw it when you are enveloped from head to foot in sweeping robes must be well-nigh impossible.

This second visit passed more cheerfully than the first. The fresh mountain wind had blown away the mists of ceremony, there was no interpreter between us, and we had a common interest on which to exchange our opinions. That is the secret of agreeable conversation. It is not originality which charms; even wit ceases in the end to provoke a smile. The true pleasure is to recount your own doings to your fellow-man, and if by a lucky chance you find that he has been doing precisely the same thing, and is therefore able to listen and reply with understanding, no further bond is needed for perfect friendship. Unfortunately, this tie was lacking between us and the monkey, who was also in villeggiatura by the banks of the Lar, and in consequence we got no further forward with him than before. Our presence seemed, indeed, to exasperate him more than ever. He spent the time of our visit making spiteful dashes at us, in the vain hope that the gods might in the end reward his perseverance and lengthen his chain sufficiently to allow him to bite us but once before we left.

But the gods have eternity in their hand, and we must hasten, for our time is short; long ere the monkey's prayer was answered we had risen and taken leave of the three ladies. We left them gazing after us from behind their canvas walls. Their prisoned existence seemed to us a poor mockery of life as we cantered homewards up the damp valley, the mountain air sending a cheerful warmth through our veins. The thunderstorm was past, the sun dropped in clear splendour behind the mountains, leaving a red glory to linger on the slopes of Demavend, and bearing the fulness of his light to the Western world—to our own world.

THE TREASURE OF THE KING

CHOLERA had swept through Tehran since last we set foot in its streets, and they seemed to us more than usually empty and deserted in the vacant sunshine that autumn morning. But the Ark, the centre and heart of the city, was crowded still. Though many of the tiny shops had been closed by owners whose own account had been closed summarily and for ever, the people who remained went about their business as cheerfully as before, gesticulated over their bargains, drew their long robes round them in dignified disgust as we passed, and sipped their glasses of tea with unimpaired enjoyment. The motley crowd was yet further diversified by the scarlet coats of the Shah's farrashes, the many-coloured garments and fantastic head-gear of the servants of the palace, and the ragged uniforms of the soldiers who hung about the street corners—an army scarcely more efficient, I should imagine, than its rudely-painted counterpart upon the walls. These rough drawings satisfy the eye and tickle the artistic taste of the King of Kings. He is not difficult to please. Take a wooden soldier for model (carefully omitting his little green stand), magnify him to the size of life, put the brightest colours into his uniform and his cheeks, and you will be furnished with a design which is considered worthy of decorating not only the principal gateways of Tehran, but all the streets leading to the palace.

In Eastern life there are no modulations. As the day leaps suddenly into night with no warning time of twilight, so, to adapt the words of Omar the Tent-Maker, between the house of riches and of penury there is but a breath. We were accustomed to strange contrasts, yet it scarcely seemed possible that this gaudy squalor could be the setting of the priceless Treasure of the King. The stories we had heard of its magnificence must be due to the fecundity of the Oriental imagination. The East is the birthplace of wonders; there the oft-repeated tale gains a semblance of veracity which ends by deceiving not only credulous listeners, but him also who invented it. We should have received it like other fairy stories, sedulously nursing the happy faith which flies all opportunity of proving itself a superstition.

We stopped before an unregal gateway, and were conducted with much ceremony into the palace. The palace was unexpectedly beautiful, after all. Crossing a narrow strip of garden, we found ourselves in its first court—a court of Government offices, we were told, though the word *office* conveys no impression of the graceful buildings, from the upper galleries of which curtains floated, fanning the air within to coolness. Our guides led us beneath more archways, through high, dark passages, and out into the sunlight of the central garden. It was built round with an irregular architecture. Here the walls were radiant with faïence, there a row of arches stood back from the sun-beaten pavement—delicate arches which might have graced some quiet Italian cloister—beyond them stood the much-decorated building where the Shah sits in state on the day of the New Year, and which was separated from the garden in front only by the folds of an immense curtain, which, when it is drawn back, discloses the carved throne set in a grove of columns. Still further on we reached the palace itself, two-storied and many-windowed, from whose steps stretched the dainty pleasure-grounds, with their paved paths and smooth, fresh grass, their trees and gay flower-beds, between which fountains leapt joyfully, and streams meandered over their blue-tiled beds. They were bounded by the impenetrable and forbidding walls of the andarun.

Mounting the marble staircase, we found ourselves before a big wooden doorway, the seal on whose lock had to be broken ere it could be thrown open to us. We stood expectantly while the Minister, our guide, fumbled at the lock. Perhaps he was really some powerful efreet whom, after long captivity, our presence had released from the bottle in which Solomon had prisoned him. We were half prepared for the fairy treasures he had come forth to reveal to us.

Prepared? Ah, no, indeed! For what sober mortal could be prepared for the sight that burst upon us?

A great vaulted room with polished floor and painted walls, with deep alcoves through whose long narrow windows splashes of sunlight fell—and everywhere jewels! Jewels on all the shelves of the alcoves, thick-sown jewels on the carpets which hung against the walls, jewels coruscating from the throne at the top of the room, jewels in glass cases down the middle, flashing and sparkling in the sunlight, gleaming through dark corners, irradiating the whole hall with their scintillant brightness. With dazzled eyes we turned to one of the alcoves, and fell to examining the contents of the shelves. Here were swords sheathed in rubies; here were wands and sceptres set from end to end with spirals of turquoise and sapphire; diamond crowns, worthy to throw a halo of light round the head of an emperor; breastplates and epaulets, from whose encrusted emeralds the spear of the enemy would glance aside, shields whose bewildering splendour would blind his eyes. Here were rings and bracelets and marvellous necklaces, stars and orders and undreamt-of ornaments, and, as though the ingenuity of the goldsmiths had been exhausted before they had reached the end of their task, rows and rows of tiny glasses filled with unset stones — diamonds, sapphires, topazes, amethysts—the nectar of an Olympian god frozen in the cup. Under glass cases lay the diadems of former kings, high, closed helmets ablaze with precious stones; masses of unstrung pearls; costly and hideous toys, remarkable only for their extraordinary value — a globe, for instance, supported by an unbroken column of diamonds, whose seas were made of great flat emeralds, and whose continents of rubies and sapphires; and scattered with lavish profusion among the cases, festoons of turquoise rings and broad gold pieces which have long passed out of use, but in which regal currency, it is related, an immense subsidy was once paid to the Czar. On the other side of the room the treasures were scarcely less valuable and even more beautiful, for cupboard after cupboard was filled with delicate enamel, bowls and flagons, and the stems of kalyans all decorated with exquisite patterns in the soft blended colours whose freshness is immortal. These lay far beyond the criticism of captious connoisseurs, who would not have failed to point out to us that the jewels were tinsel-backed, after all, and that most of the enormous rose diamonds were flawed and discoloured.

Taking an honoured place among the

jewels and the enamel there were some objects which raised a ripple of laughter in the midst of our admiration. The royal owner of the treasure-house, doubtless anxious to show that he considered no less the well-being of the inward than the adornment of the outward man, had filled some of his upper shelves with little bottles of—— what could those silvery globules be? we wondered, gazing curiously upwards. Not white enough for pearls, and yet they could not be, though they looked suspiciously like —yes, they were!—they were pills! Yes, indeed they were pills — quack remedies which the Shah had collected on his Western travels, had brought home and placed among his treasures. After this discovery we were not surprised to find bottles of cheap scents and of tooth-powder among the diamonds, nor to observe that some of the priceless cloisonné bowls were filled with toothbrushes; nor was it even a disillusion when we were solemnly told that the wooden cases placed at intervals down the room, each on its small table, were only musical boxes, which it is the delight of the Protector of the Universe to set a-playing all at once when he comes to inspect his treasures. Heaven knows by what fortunate combination of circumstances he finds those treasures still intact, for they seemed to us very insufficiently guarded, unless the tutelary efreet watches over them. There is, indeed, a locked door, of which the King and the Prime Minister alone possess a key; but a thief is not usually deterred by the necessity of forcing a lock, and if a scrupulous sense of honour prevented him from breaking the royal seal, with a little ingenuity he might contrive an entrance through one of the many windows, or even through the roof, were he of an enterprising disposition; and once within, nothing but the glass cupboard-doors would separate him from riches so vast that he might carry away a fortune without fear of detection.

We were next taken to see the world-famous Peacock Throne, which is reported to have been brought from Delhi by a conquering Shah. A scarlet carpet sewn with pearls covered its floor, on which the King sits cross-legged in Eastern fashion, surrounded by a blaze of enamel and precious stones. A year ago this throne had been the centre of a hideous story of cupidity and palace intrigue — who can tell what forgotten crimes have invested its jewels with their cruel, tempting glitter? We passed on into a long succession of charming rooms with low, painted ceilings, walls covered with a mosaic of looking-glass, and windows facing the smiling garden. Execrable copies of the very worst European pictures adorned them; one was hung with framed photographs—groups taken on the Shah's travels, in which his shabby figure occupied a prominent place, and all wearing that inane vacuity of expression which is characteristic of photographic groups, whether they be of royal personages or of charity school children. Here and there a wonderful carpet lent its soft glow to the rooms, but for the most part the floors were covered with coarse productions of European looms — those flaming roses, and vulgar, staring patterns, which exercise an unfortunate attraction over the debased Oriental taste of to-day.

With a feeling of hopeless bewilderment, we at length quitted the palace where we had been dazzled by inconceivable wealth and moved to ridicule by childish folly. Wealth and childishness seemed to us equally absurd as we rode home in silence along the dusty roads.

Before our garden gates there dwelt a holy dervish. He, too, was a king—in the realms of poverty—and over the narrow strip of wilderness he bore undisputed sway. He levied pious alms for taxes, his palace was a roof of boughs, four bare poles were the columns of his throne, and the stones of the desert his crown jewels. His days were spent in a manner which differed little from that of his neighbour and brother sovereign. The whole long summer through he had collected the surrounding stones and piled them into regular heaps. His futile religious exercise was almost completed, he was putting the finishing touches to a work which winter winds and snows would as surely destroy as the winter of ill-fortune will scatter the other's wealth. But the dervish was untroubled by thoughts of the future; he laboured to the glory of God in his own strange fashion, and though his jewels needed neither locks nor seals nor men-at-arms to guard them, their human interest lent them a value unattained by the Treasure of the King.

SHEIKH HASSAN

I USED to watch him coming round the curve of the avenue, his quick step somewhat impeded by the long robes he wore, holding his cloak round him with one hand, his head bent down, and his eyes fixed on the ground. As he drew near he would glance up, wrinkling his eyebrows in the effort to pierce the darkness of the great tent under which I was sitting. The plane-trees grew straight and tall on each side of the road; overhead their branches touched one another, arching together and roofing it with leaves fresh and green, as only plane-leaves can be all through the hot summer. Between the broad leaves fell tiny circles of sunshine, which flickered on his white turban and on the linen vest about his throat as he came. He looked like a very part of his surroundings, for his woollen cloak was of a faded gray, the colour of Persian dust, and his under-robe was as green as the plane-leaves, and his turban gleamed like the sunshine; but his face was his own, brown and keen, with dark eyes, deep-set under the well-marked brows, and his thin brown hands were his own too, and instinct with character. If you had only seen the hands, you might fairly have hazarded a guess at the sort of man he was, for they were thoughtful hands, delicate and nervous, with thin wrists, on which the veins stood out, and long fingers, rather blunt at the tips; and the skin, which was a shade darker than the sun can tan, would have told you he was an Oriental. I believe he came up from Tehran on a mule on the days appointed for our lesson, and reached our village at some incredibly early hour in order to avoid the morning heat; but the six-mile journey must have been disagreeable at best, for the roads were ankle-deep in dust, and the sun blazed fiercely almost as soon as it was above the horizon. The cool shaded garden and the dark tent, with an overflowing tank in the midst of it, and a stream of fresh water running over the blue tiles in front, was a welcome refuge after the close heat of the town and the dusty ride.

'Peace be with you!' he would say with a low bow. 'Is the health of your Excellency good?' 'Thanks be to God, it is very good,' I would answer. 'Thanks be to God!' he would return piously, with another bow. Then he would draw up a chair and sit down in front of me, folding his hands under his wide sleeves, crossing his white-stockinged feet, and gazing round him with his bright quick eyes. He made use of no gestures while he talked, his hands remained folded and his feet crossed, and only his keen, restless glances and the sudden movements round the corners of his lips told when he was interested. He never laughed, though he smiled often, and his smile was enigmatical, and betokened not so much amusement as indulgent surprise at the curious views of Europeans. I often wondered what thoughts there were, lurking in his brain, that brought that odd curl round the corners of his mouth, but I never arrived at any certainty as to what was passing through his mind, except that sometimes he was indubitably bored, and was longing that the lesson were over, and that he might be permitted to go and sleep through the hot hours. On these occasions he expressed his feelings by yawns, very long and very frequent — it certainly was hot! I was often sleepy too, for I had been up and out riding quite as early as he.

Our intercourse was somewhat restricted by the fact that we had no satisfactory medium through which to convey our thoughts to each other. He spoke French—such French as is to be acquired at Tehran! and I—ah well! I fear my Persian never carried me very far. Nevertheless, we were accustomed to embark recklessly on the widest discussions. He was a bit of a reformer was Sheikh Hassan; indeed, he had got himself into trouble with the Government on more occasions than one by a too open expression of his opinions, and the modern equivalent for the bow-string had perhaps flicked nearer his shoulders than he quite liked; a free-thinker too, and a sceptic to the tips of his brown fingers. A quatrain of Omar Khayyam's would plunge us into the deepest waters of philosophic uncertainty, with not even the poor raft of a common tongue to float us over, from whence we would emerge, gasping and coughing, with a mutual respect for each other's linguistic efforts, but small knowledge of what they were intended to convey. Pity that such a gulf lay between us, though I dare say it came to much the same in the end, for, as Hafiz has remarked in another metaphor, ' To no man's wisdom those grim gates stand open, or will ever stand!'

The Sheikh had an unlimited contempt for Persian politics. ' It is all rotten!' he would say—' rotten! rotten! What would you have?' (with a lifting of the eyebrows). ' We are all corrupt, and the Shah is our lord. You would have to begin by sweeping away everything that exists.' But his disbelief in the efficacy of European civilization was equally profound, and his pessimism struck me as being further sighted than the careless optimism of those who seek to pile one edifice upon another, a Western upon an Eastern world, and never pause to consider whether, if it stands at all, the newer will only stand by crushing the older out of all existence. Sheikh Hassan, at all events, was not very hopeful. 'Triste pays!' he would say at the end of such a conversation. 'Ah, triste pays!' and though I knew he had his own views as to the possible future of his country, he was far too discreet a man to confide them to frivolous ears.

Concerning his private life I never liked to question him, though I would have given much to know what his own household was like. He had a wife and children down in Tehran. The good lady looked with unmitigated disapproval upon infidel foreigners, and her husband was obliged to conceal from her how many hours of the day he spent with them. Judging by an anecdote I heard of her during the cholera time, she must have ruled the establishment with a hand of iron. The Sheikh, being much concerned over the risk his family was running in the plague-stricken town, had taken the precaution of laying in six bottles of brandy, the most convenient medicine he could obtain, and hearing at the same time that a good bargain offered itself in the matter of olive-oil, he, as a prudent man, had also purchased six bottles of oil and stored them too in his cellar. But on one luckless morning, when his wife happened to enter there, she espied the brandy lurking in a dark corner. Being a lady of marked religious convictions, she at once called to mind the words which the Prophet has pronounced against alcoholic liquors, and without more ado opened the bottles and poured out their contents upon the floor. On further search her eldest daughter discovered the oil in another corner. Having observed the conduct of her mother, she concluded that she could not do better than imitate it, and accordingly the innocent liquid also streamed out over the cellar floor, libation to an unheeding god. The unfortunate Sheikh found on his return that his foresight and his skill in bargaining had alike been brought to nought by the misguided fervour of the female members of his family. To none of them did the cholera prove fatal, though the wife suffered from a slight attack; but Sheikh Hassan spent anxious weeks until the danger was over. 'For thirty-seven nights,' he told me pathetically, 'I lay awake and considered what could be done for my children's safety.' With true Oriental fatalism, he did not seem to have taken any active steps in the matter, and at the end of his thirty-seven nights of thought he was as far from any conclusion as ever. Happily, the extreme fury of the cholera had by that time abated.

The mysteries of Eastern education were no less unfathomable to me. Though he was a man of middle age, Sheikh Hassan had only recently quitted the Madrasseh, a sort of religious college, of which he had been a student. There he had been taught Arabic, geography and astronomy; he had read some philosophy too, for he was acquainted, in a translation, with the works of Aristotle, and he had learnt much concerning the doctrines of religion, which study had profited him little, since he heartily disbelieved in them all. He wrote a beautiful hand, and was very proud of the accomplishment. He would sharpen a reed pen and sit for half an hour writing out quatrains with elaborate care and the most exquisite flourishes, and he evinced such delight over the performance that I could not find it in my heart to interrupt him. He was very anxious that I, too, should acquire this art. I asked him how much time I should have to devote to it. 'Well,' he replied reflectively, 'if for five or six years you were to spend three hours of every day in writing, you might at the end be tolerably proficient.' He did not appear to consider that the achievement was in any way incommensurate with the labour he proposed that I should undergo, and I abstained from all criticism that might hurt his feelings. I wrote him long letters in Persian characters. 'Duste azize man,' they began—'Dear friend of mine.' He would read them during the lesson, and answer them in terms of the most elaborate politeness—'My slave was honoured by my commands,' and so forth; and my crude and uncertain lines became abhorrent to me when I saw him covering his paper with a lovely decorative design of courteous phrases. He was not without dreams of literary fame. One day he laid before me a vast scheme of collaboration: we were to compile a Persian grammar together; it would be such a grammar as the world had never seen (in which statement I fancy he came nearer the truth than he well knew!); he would write the Persian, and I should translate it into French. I agreed to all, being well assured that we should never bring our courage to the sticking point. We never did — the grammar of the Persian language is still to be written.

The one really useful piece of knowledge he possessed had not been taught him at the Madrasseh—he had picked up French by himself, he told me. I could have wished that he had picked it up in a somewhat less fragmentary condition, for his translations did but little to define the meaning of the original Persian. We read some of Hafiz together, but the Sheikh had only one gender at his disposal, and the poet's impassioned descriptions of his mistresses were always conveyed to me in the masculine. 'Boucles de cheveux' seemed at first a strange beauty in a lady, but custom, the leveller of sensations, brought me to accept without question even this Gorgon - like adornment. The Sheikh took a particular pleasure in the more philosophical verses. Over these I would puzzle for long hours, and in all innocence arrive at the conclusion that some anecdote of angels, or what not, appertaining, doubtless, to the Mohammedan religion, was related in them. The Sheikh would then proceed to annotate them in halting French, pointing out that a pun was contained in every rhyme, that half the words bore at the smallest computation two or three different meanings, and that therefore the lines might be done into several English versions, each with an entirely different significance, and each an equally truthful rendering of the Persian. At this my brain would begin to whirl. I was unable to deal with the confusion of difficulties among which the Sheikh Hassan was delightedly battling; it was enough for me if I could seize some of the beauty which lay like a sheath about the poems, the delicate, exquisite rhythm of the love-songs, the recurrent music of the rhyme, and the noble swing of the refrains. I received and admired their proud stoicism as it stood written: women were women and wine red wine for me, the cup-bearer was the person whose advent was most eagerly to be greeted; roses and nightingales, soft winds and blooming gardens, were all part of a beautiful imaginative world, and fit setting for a poet's dreams.

But this was wilful stupidity. If I had listened to the wisdom of Sheikh Hassan, I should have realized that we were in the midst of sublime abstractions, and that the most rigid morality and the strictest abstinence were inculcated by those glowing lines. In practice, however, I had the poets themselves on my side; the days of Hafiz sped merrily, if tradition has not belied him, and the last prayer of the Tent-Maker was that he might be buried in a rose-garden, where the scented petals would fall softly upon his head and remind him after his death of the joys he had loved on earth.

Were these things also abstractions?

For lighter reading we had the Shah's Diary, a work whose childlike simplicity admitted of but one interpretation. I never got through very much of it, but I read far enough to see that the royal author did not consider himself bound by the ordinary rules of literary production. He was accustomed in particular to pass from one subject to another with a rapidity which was almost breathless. The book began somewhat after this fashion: 'In the month of Sha'ban, God looked with extraordinary clemency upon the world; the crops stood high in the fields, and plenty was showered upon his fortunate people by the hand of Allah. I mounted my horse and proceeded to the review. . . .'

At last the day of parting came; with much regret I told the Sheikh I was about to leave Persia. 'Ah, well,' he replied, 'I'm very glad you are going. Healthy people should not stay here; it's not the place for healthy people.' We fell to making many plans for a meeting in England, a country he had often expressed a desire to visit, I as often assuring him that an enthusiastic reception should be his. I fear these also will never be brought to fulfilment, but if he should ever come, it would be interesting to find what peculiarities in us and in our ways would attract the notice of his bright, observant eyes. I confess it would give me no small pleasure to meet him walking along Piccadilly in his white turban and flowing robes, and to hear once more the familiar salutation: 'The health of your Excellency is good? Thanks be to God!'

A PERSIAN HOST

WE were riding. We had left Tehran the previous evening in a storm of rain and hail, which had covered the mountain-tops with their first sheet of winter snow. We had slept at a tiny post-house, sixteen miles from the city gates—an unquiet lodging it had proved, for travellers came clattering in all through the early hours of the night, and towards morning the post dashed past, changing horses and speeding forward on its way to Tabriz. The beauty of the night compensated in a measure for wakeful hours; the moon—our last Persian moon—shone out of a clear heaven, its beams glittered on the fields of freshly-fallen snow far away on the mountains, and touched with mysterious light the sleeping forms of Persian travellers stretched in rows on the ground in the veranda of the post-house. We were up before the autumn dawn, and started on our road just as the sun shot over the mountains. Ali Akbar led the way — Ali Akbar, the swiftest rider on the road to Resht, he with the surest judgment as to the merits of a post-horse, the richest store of curses for delinquent post-boys, the deftest hand in the confection of a pillau, the brightest twinkle of humour darting from under shaggy brows — friend, counsellor, protector, and incidentally our servant. He had wound a scarlet turban round his head, he made it a practice not to wash on a journey, and his usually shaven beard had begun to assume alarming proportions before we reached the Caspian. His saddle-bags and his huge pockets bulged with miscellaneous objects—a cake, a pot of marmalade, a crossed Foreign Office bag, a saucepan, a pair of embroidered slippers which he had produced in the rain and presented to us a mile or two from Tehran, with a view, I imagine, to establishing the friendliest relations between us. We followed; in the rear came two baggage-horses carrying our scanty luggage, and driven by a mounted post-boy, generally deficient. These three, the baggage-horses and the post-boy, were our weak point—a veritable heel of Achilles; they represented to us 'black Care,' which is said to follow behind every horseman. What a genius those horses had for tumbling over stones! What a limitless capacity for sleep was possessed by those post-boys! How easily could the Gordian knot have been unloosed if its ropes had shared in the smallest measure that feeling for simplicity which animated those which bound our baggage!

The first stage that morning was pleasant enough; then came the heat and the dust with it. Sunshine—sunshine! tedious, changeless, monotonous! Not that discreet English sunshine which varies its charm with clouds, with rainbows, with golden mist, as an attractive woman varies her dress and the fashion of her hair—'ever afresh and ever anew,' as the Persian poet has it—here the sun has long ceased trying to please so venerable a world. The long straight road lay ahead; the desolate plain stretched southwards, mile after uninterrupted mile; the bare mountain barrier shut out the north; and for sound, the thud of our horses' feet as we rode, the heavy, tired thud of cantering feet, and the gasp of the indrawn breath, for as the stage drew to its close the weary beasts cantered on more and more sullenly through dust and heat.

At last far away, where the road dipped and turned, stood the longed-for clump of trees, clustered round the great caravanserai and the glittering blue-tiled dome of the little mosque. This was not an ordinary post-house, but a stately pile, four-square, built by some pious person in the reign of Shah Abbas, and the mosque was the shrine and tomb of a saint, a descendant of the Prophet. Behind it lay a huge mound of earth, a solid watch-tower heaped up in turbulent times. From its summit the anxious inhabitants of the caravanserai could see far and wide over the plain, and shut their gates betimes before an on-coming foe. . . . War has passed away round the shrine of the Yengi Imam, yet it is not security, but indifference, that is high-priest under the blue dome, and though the shadows of the old watchers gazing from the earth-heap would see no sturdy band of Persian robbers rushing down on them from the mountains, they may tremble some day before a white-capped Russian army, marching resistless along the dusty road.

The clatter of the post-horses over the stones broke the noon-day silence. Yengi Imam looked very desolate and uncared-for as we rode through the mud-heaps before its hospitable doors. Half the blue tiles had fallen from the dome, unnoticed and unreplaced, meagre poplars shivered in the sun, stunted pomegranate bushes carpeted the ground with yellow autumn leaves, their heavy dark-red fruit a poor exchange for the spring glory of crimson flower. Persians love pomegranates, and on a journey prize them above all other fruits, and even to the foreigner their pink fleshy pips, thick set like jewels, are not without charm. But it is mainly the charm of the imagination and of memories of Arabian Night stories in which disguised princes ate preserved pomegranate seeds, and found them delicious. Do not attempt to follow their example, for when you have tasted the essence of steel knife with which a pomegranate is flavoured, you will lose all confidence in the judgment of princes, even in disguise. And it is a pity to destroy illusions. But for beauty give me pomegranate bushes in the spring, with dark, dark green leaves and glowing flowers, thick and pulpy like a fruit, and winged with delicate petals, red as flame.

Through the low door of the caravanserai we entered the cool vault of the stable which ran all round the garden court. A lordly stable it was, lighted by shafts of sunshine falling from the glass balls with which each tiny dome was studded—vault beyond vault, dusty light and shadowy darkness following each other in endless succession till the eye lost itself in the flickering sunshine of a corner dome. Here stood weary post-horses, sore-backed and broken-kneed; here lay piles of sweet-smelling hay and heaped-up store of grain. At one corner was a minute bazaar, where we could buy thin flaps of bread if we had a mind to eat flour mixed in equal parts with sand and fashioned into the semblance of brown paper; raisins also, and dried figs, bunches of black grapes, sweet and good, and tiny glasses of weak hot tea, much sugared, which pale amber-coloured beverage is more comforting to the traveller on burning Persian roads than the choicest of the forbidden juices of the grape. The great stable enclosed a square plot of garden — orchard, rather, for it was all planted with fruit-trees — which, after the manner of Eastern gardens, was elaborately watered by a network of rivulets flowing into a large central tank, roofed over to protect it from the sun. He did his work well, the pious founder of the caravanserai, but he thought more of the comfort of beasts than of men. One or two bare rooms opening into the garden, a few windowless, airless holes in the inner wall, a row of dark niches above the mangers — that was what he judged to be good enough for such as he; the high, cool domes were for weary horses and tinkling caravans of mules.

We were well content to stretch ourselves in the mules' palace with a heap of their hay for bed. Thirty-two miles of road lay behind us, thirty-two miles in front — an hour's rest at mid-day did not come amiss.

As we lay we saw in the garden a Persian, dressed in the pleated frock-coat and the tall brimless astrakhan hat which are the customary clothes of a gentleman. Round his hat was wrapped a red scarf to protect it from the dust of travelling; the rest of his attire was as spotless as though dust were an unknown quantity to him. He watched us attentively for some minutes, and then beckoned us to his room opposite. We rose, still stiff from the saddle, and walked slowly round the court. He greeted us with the calm dignity of bearing that sits as easily on the Oriental as his flowing robes. Manner and robe would be alike impossible in the busy breathless life of the West, where, if you pause for a moment even to gird your loins, half your competitors have passed you before you look up. The Oriental holds aloof, nor are the folds of his garments disturbed by any unseemly activity. He stands and waits the end; his day is past. There is much virtue in immobility if you take the attitude like a philosopher, yet to fade away gracefully is a difficult task for men or nations—the mortal coil is apt to entangle departing feet and compromise the dignity of the exit.

'Salaam uleikum!' said our new friend—

'Peace be with you!' and, taking us by the hand, he led us into his room, which was furnished with a mat and a couple of wooden bedsteads. On one of these he made us sit, and set out before us on a sheet of bread a roast chicken, an onion, some salt, a round ball of cheese, and some bunches of grapes; then, seeing that we hesitated as to the proper mode of attacking the chicken, he took it in his fingers, delicately pulled apart wings, legs and breast, and motioned us again to eat. He himself was provided with another, to which he at once turned his attention, and thus encouraged, we also fell to. Never did roast chicken taste so delicious! I judge from other experiences that he was probably tough; he was, alas! small, but, for all that, we look back to him with gratitude as having furnished the most excellent luncheon we ever ate. In ten minutes his bones, the onion, and a pile of grape skins were the only traces left of our repast, and we got up feeling that two more stages on tired post-horses were as nothing in the length of a September afternoon.

We said farewell to our unknown host, stammering broken phrases of polite Persian. 'Out of his great kindness we had eaten an excellent breakfast; the clemency of his nobility was excessive; we hoped that he might carry himself safely to Tehran, and that God would be with him.' But though our Persian was poor, gratitude shone from our faces. He bowed and smiled, and assured us that our servant was honoured by our having partaken of his chicken, but he would not shake hands with us because he had not yet washed his fingers, which, as he had used them as knives and forks both for himself and for us, were somewhat sticky.

So we mounted our horses, and rode away

towards our crude Western world, and he mounted his and passed eastward into his own cities. Who he is, and what his calling, we shall never know—nor would we. He remains to us a type, a charming memory, of the hospitality, the courtesy, of the East. Whether he be prince or soldier or simple traveller, God be with him! Khuda hafez—God be his Protector!

A STAGE AND A HALF

'As music at the close is sweetest last,' says Shakespeare. We cling regretfully to the close, but the beginning is what is worth having — the beginning, with all its freshness, all its enthusiasm, all its unexpected charm, Hercules for strength, Atalanta for speed, Gabriel for fair promise. Say what you will, the end is sad. Do not linger over the possibilities to which (all unfulfilled) it sets a term, but remember the glorious energy which spurred you forward at first, and which lies ready to spring forth anew.

When we were riding post, we had occasion to study the philosophy of beginnings. 'Ah, if we could only have gone on like that!' we sighed when, finding ourselves at the end of a weary day only thirty miles removed from our starting-point, we remembered the sixty flashing miles that had passed beneath our horses' feet the day before. The long road to the sea seemed an eternity of space not to be measured by our creeping, tired steps. Yet with the dawn our views had changed. However weary, however stiff you may be when in the dusk you reach the last half-farsakh of the last half-stage, the night's rest will send you on with as keen a pleasure as if you had been lying idle for a week before. The clear day, the low cool sun, the delicious cup of tea flavoured with the morning, the fresh horse, the long straight road in front of you —away! away! A careful jog, a steady canter, who does not feel that he could put a girdle round the earth at the beginning of the first stage? And then the sun creeps higher, shadows and mists vanish, the dust dances in the hot road, your horse jogs on more slowly—how large the world is, how long four farsakhs! And beyond them lie another four, and yet another; better not to think of them — Inshallah, we shall sleep somewhere to-night!

Through all these vicissitudes of mood we were destined to pass on the second day of our riding. The sun was already high when we reached the city which lay at the end of our first stage, and passed under its tiled gateway into a wide street, a good half of whose mud houses were so ruinous that they can have fulfilled none of the objects for which houses are erected. As we penetrated further into the city, the streets narrowed and became more populous—thronged, indeed, with long-robed men and shrouded women, buying and selling, eating fruit, chatting before the barbers' shops, scowling at us as they moved out of our way. We rode down a wide tree-planted avenue, bordered by houses gaily patterned with coloured bricks, past the hammam where the coarse blue towels were stretched in line against the wall to dry, past the beautiful gateway of the Prince's palace, under whose arch of blue and green and yellow faïence we could see the cool garden set with trees and fountains. Presently we were lying in a little alcove under the archway of a tiny tumble-down post-house, vainly demanding fresh horses. Stray Persians sat round in the street, eating grapes and bread, drinking water out of earthen pitchers, watching us with grave, observant faces, quite unmoved by our expostulations and entreaties. There was a mythical mail in front of us which had swept away an incredible number of horses—seventeen or eighteen, the owner of the post-house assured us; indeed, he had none left. We had heard of this mail before —all our difficulties and discomforts were in turn attributed to it. No one could explain what made the bags so unusually heavy, but I fancy such an obstacle is not infrequent on Persian roads. At any rate, the postmaster was not mistaken when he foretold our disbelief of his statements.

At length we were off again at the very hottest moment of the day. At the town gate the baggage-horses turned homesick, and refused to move any further from their ruined stalls; in despair we left Ali Akbar to deal with them and rode on alone. On and on slowly through endless vineyards, past an evil-smelling cemetery where the cholera had dug many rows of fresh graves; on and on till the signs of habitation that encircled the town had disappeared, and we found ourselves in a bare, flat, desolate land. A keen wind rose, and blew from the mountains wreaths of storm-cloud which eclipsed the sun, and still there was no sign of the little town which marked the next half-stage. We looked round us in complete ignorance of our whereabouts, and espied in the distance a village walled round with crenellated mud, in front of whose gates some children were playing. Riding up to them, we inquired whether we were on the right road. Alas! we were not. Unperceived, it had trended away northwards, and heaven knows to what dim cities we were diligently riding! So we turned northwards, directed by a barely defined track through the wilderness.

Just as the storm began to break we met a blue-robed pedlar with a merry face, who assured us that we had only half an hour further to go. He, too, was making for

Agababa; he had seen our nobilities lying in the post-house at Kasvin — yes, it was only a thin farsakh more now. At length, through wind and rain, we reached the vineyards and gardens of Agababa, and passed under the shelter of its big gate-house. Here we determined to lodge, deciding that on such a night further progress was out of the question. We turned to the people who were gathered under the archway, talking and smoking kalyans, and asked them whose house this was. It belonged to Hadgi Abdullah, the Shah's farrash. We intimated that we wished to lodge here — where was Hadgi Abdullah? He was in Tehran, they replied, but offered no suggestion as to the course we should pursue. We left them to smoke their kalyans in peace, and, taking the matter into our own hands, we dismounted, ordered tea and fire, and climbed the steep staircase that led into the balakhaneh. It consisted of three rooms: a large one in the centre, with a long low window of tiny panes set in delicate but broken woodwork, and opening on to a balcony; on either side two smaller rooms, one of which was furnished with a carpet and inhabited by two Persians, while the other was completely empty except for some walnuts spread out to dry in one corner. Here we established ourselves, to the entire unconcern of the Persians, who treated the sudden invasion of their quarters by two damp and muddy travellers as a matter not worthy of remark. Half an hour later Ali Akbar joined us. We interrogated him as to the probable fate of the baggage. He replied, laying his head upon his clasped hands, that the horses were most likely asleep, which seemed so reasonable an explanation from what we had seen of their disposition that it did not occur to us to inquire why no steps had been taken to have them awakened. But the valiant Ali Akbar was not to be daunted by the unpromising aspect of things. Borrowing a brazier, he began to cook us a meal, a process which we impeded by vainly attempting to dry our clothes over the glowing charcoal, for our own fire smoked so abominably that it was not possible to stay in the same room with it, and in self-defence we were obliged to let it go out. It was a glad moment when our supper was set before us, for since the cake and tea of the early morning we had eaten nothing, and the chicken, the eggs, and the boiled rice (which had been filched from the evening meal of some inhabitant of Agababa) looked most appetising. Moreover, the same obliging person — he was a ragged muleteer, whose feet had been developed to an abnormal size either by much travelling or by the necessity of kicking his mules to drive them onward—had provided us with a large dish of delicious grapes.

The servants of the palace are not, unfortunately, numbered among our friends, and it seems improbable that we shall ever make the acquaintance of Hadgi Abdullah, but we remain eternally his debtors for the night's shelter his roof afforded us. His hospitality went no further than a roof—we spread our own cloaks for beds, our own saddles served us for pillows, and for our dinner we went a-foraging—but though his floor was hard, though his fire smoked, though his walnuts stained our elbows when we leant on them, though the bond of bread and salt is not between us, still that unknown pilgrim was a benefactor to us pilgrims of a more distant land than holy Mecca. How does he spend his days, I wonder, in that Agababa gate-house of his, where for one stormy autumn night we rested? Does he fly to his peaceful, mud-walled village from time to time when the service of the palace has become hateful to him? Does he sit at sunset on the balcony overlooking his laden fruit-trees, smoking a kalyan, and watching the village folk as they drive home the flocks of goats under his archway—as they stagger through it loaded with wood bundles? And when the sun has set behind the sweeping curve of mountains, what peaceful thoughts of the future, of restful age, of projects accomplished, come to him with the sweet smell of wood fires and of savoury evening meals?

Ah, simple pleasures, so familiar in a land so far removed! Not in great towns, not in palaces, had we felt the tie of humanity which binds East and West, but in that distant roadside village, lying on the floor of the Shah's farrash, we claimed kinship with the toilers of an alien soil. For one night we, too, were taking our share in their lives, with one flash of insight the common link of joy and sorrow was revealed to us— to us of a different civilization and a different world.

So we lay and listened to the wind, and slept a little; but a waterproof is not the best of mattresses, and our beds were passing hard. Moreover, the good pilgrim had neglected the sweeping of his floors for some time previously, and there were many strange inhabitants of the dust besides ourselves. In the middle of the night news was brought that our baggage had passed us and gone on to the end of the stage; an hour or two later we rose and followed it, with the keen storm-wind still blowing in our faces. A late waning moon shone brilliantly over our heads, and behind the house of Hadgi Abdullah lay the first white streaks of the day.

A BRIDLE-PATH

WHEN we saw the post-house of Mazreh, where we rejoined our missing baggage, we rejoiced that not under its roof, but under the hospitable roof of Hadgi Abdullah, we had taken shelter through the windy night. It was more than common dirty: the mud floors were littered with eggshells and with nameless horrors, which spoke of a yet more uneasy lodging than that of the previous evening. It stood some little way from the village of Mazreh, which lay on the lower slopes of the mountains, and beyond it our path turned upwards and was lost in the mist that hid the top of the pass.

In a year or two this bridle-path across the hills will have joined the long roll of things that were; no more will travellers entering Persia climb the narrow track which was the Shah's highway; no more will their horses' feet slip among pools of mud and ring out against the solid rock; the Russian Government have taken the highroad to Tehran into their hands, and are even now constructing a broad carriage-way from the Caspian to join the Persian road at Kasvin. But the bridle-path, which had served generations of travellers before us, had a charm of its own, too—the charm of all such tracks which lead you, as it were, through the very heart of a country as uncivilized as when the waters first retreated from the hill-tops. A foot on either side of you the mountains rise in steep slopes and walls of rock, or fall into deep valleys and precipices. The narrow way seems to vanish into wilderness as you pass over it, but when you look ahead you see it running between Scylla and Charybdis, clear and secure.

The post-horses of Mazreh matched the accommodation it offered. We spent an hour listening to Ali Akbar condemning the father of the postmaster to eternal fire, and at the end found ourselves provided with sorry beasts, the merest apologies for horses, to which animals they bore but a blurred resemblance. A few hundred yards up the hill, however, we met a man driving some laden beasts, and cajoled him so successfully that he consented to exchange baggage-horses with us, whereupon we went gaily onwards, leaving him to his fate. In all probability he is still toiling towards Kasvin, with his own goods and the skins of our horses upon his shoulders.

Our path breasted the hillside boldly, and we were presently buried in a cold mist, which seemed to us all the colder after the dust and heat of the last two days in the plain. The mist lay thickly round us at the top of the pass; we pushed on at a good pace until we caught sight of a solitary tree which grows just above the hollow, where, somewhat sheltered from winter winds and snows, lies the village of Kharzan, a tiny citadel girt round with mud walls. Only half the stage was done, but we stopped at the caravanserai to breathe our horses after the long pull.

The gateway of a caravanserai is lined within on either side by a narrow platform, on which you can sit enjoying rest and shelter, smoking your kalyan and drinking your cup of tea. At Kharzan a wood-fire was burning merrily upon the bricks of one of these platforms; various Persians who were cooking and warming themselves over it made room for us when they saw us approaching, and gave us steaming glasses of tea, which we drank gratefully. There was a good deal of coming and going through the archway: laden donkeys and men wrapped in coats of sheepskin over their blue cotton garments appeared suddenly out of the mist and disappeared as suddenly into it; the crackling sticks sent bright jets of firelight flickering over wild faces and the rough coats of men and animals.

Leaving Kharzan, we turned down the pass between mountain sides bare now after the summer's scorching, but where in the spring we had seen masses of scarlet tulips in full bloom. The lower slopes in spring and autumn are covered with the black tent roofs and yellow reed walls of nomads driving their flocks from lowland pastures up to mountain-tops when the snow melts, and back to the valleys when the winter returns. But the season was well advanced when we passed, and the mountains were already deserted.

As we descended, slipping down steep places and stumbling over shelving rocks, the sun began to play that old game of his by which he loves to prove himself superior to wind and storms. We loosened and finally stripped off waterproofs, coats and cloaks, and fastened them behind our saddles; but nothing would satisfy him—he blazed more and more furiously upon the narrow, open path and upon the walls of rock and upon us, until we regretted the chill mist which still lay upon the Kharzan Pass behind us. At length we reached the bottom of the hill and crossed a stony river-bed, overgrown with tamarisk bushes, at the further side of which stood a post-house, with some fig-trees in front of it. The post-house of Paichenar is not an agreeable resting-place. It is a 'murmurous haunt of flies' even on late autumn afternoons: flies are served up with your roast chicken, flies flavour your pillau, flies swim in your wine, they buzz through the tiny rooms, and creep up the white-washed walls, regardless of the caustic references to their presence which are written up in all languages by travellers whose patience they have tried beyond endurance. Flies are so illiterate; not one of those many tongues appeals to them.

We ate our mid-day meal in their company, and set off again towards Menjil, following the course of the river—a long stage through burning afternoon sun and the cold chill of dusk, before we reached the Valley of the White River. Menjil has an unhonoured name among Persian villages; it is reputed to be the windiest place in all the Iranian Empire. Morning, noon and night the wind whistles round its mud-houses — that they stand at all must be due only to the constant interposition of Providence in their favour, and even so they stand in a most dilapidated condition. It blows the branches of the olive-trees all to one side, making them look like stunted people breasting the elements, with their hair streaming out behind them; it lashes the swift current of the Sefid Rud. until its waters seem to turn backward and beat in waves against the lower side of the bridge piers. By the time we caught sight of the twinkling lights of the village, we felt as though we had traversed every climate the world has to offer, beginning with the frigid zone in the morning, and crossing the equator in the afternoon, to say nothing of a long evening ride through the second circle of the Inferno and the 'Bufera infernal che mai non resta.'

It was dark as we plashed through the stream which runs between the low houses as you approach Menjil, almost too dark to avoid trampling on the children who were playing along it, and the homeward plodding goats which stepped suddenly out of the night. We knew our way, however, and turned up from the water (not without a curious sensation of surprise at our own intimacy with that small and remote Persian village) into the main street, where the post-house and the telegraph-office stand. The post-house, where we had slept before on our outward journey, was comfortable enough as post-houses go—it was even furnished with some luxury, for it boasted a wooden table and some chairs. There was a Russian family in possession when we arrived, father, mother, and a troop of children, who were making their way down to Enzeli; but they did not discommode us, as they appeared to be content with one room, and resigned the other two to us. They had left Tehran some days before us, but had travelled very slowly, the women and children going at a footpace, either slung in covered panniers across the backs of mules, or carried in a box-shaped litter, which, as it crossed hills and valleys, jolted them first on to their feet and then on to their heads in a manner which must have been disturbing to the most equable of temperaments.

We went to the telegraph-office, where we sent and received messages, profiting by the opportunity of being once more in touch with the world of men. The telegraph clerk was an agreeable Persian, who entertained us with cups of tea while we delivered our messages. His office was hung round with curtains, behind which we could hear much chattering and laughing going forward in subdued tones, and between the folds we caught from time to time glimpses of the inquisitive, laughing faces of his womenkind. What with the tea and the laughing women and the conversation of the clerk, the sending of telegrams becomes an amusing pastime in Menjil.

Next day, when we descended into the street, we found our servant engaged in heaping objurgations upon the head of a European who was sullenly watching the saddling of our fresh mounts. We inquired as to the cause of difference between them, and were informed by Ali Akbar that the man—he was an Austrian merchant—had attempted to suborn the people of the post-house, and to purloin our horses while we slept.

'And when you would have reached the parakhod (steamer),' said Ali Akbar, 'Allah alone knows, for there are no other horses fit for your Excellencies to ride!'

The stables must have been passing ill supplied, for our Excellencies had not been accustomed to show a very critical spirit in the matter of horseflesh.

'Does he also wish to reach the parakhod?' we asked in sympathetic tones.

'He is the son of a dog!' Ali Akbar replied laconically, upon which we felt that the subject might fitly be brought to a close.

The Austrian did not appear on the steamer, from which we argued that he had not succeeded in securing post-horses, after having been baffled in his attempt to ride away on ours.

We rode all the morning along a rocky little path, following the downward course of the Sefid Rud. The river where the bridge of Menjil crosses it presents an aspect extraordinarily wild and beautiful. The deep, bare valley below the bridge opens out above it into wider ground, bordered by rugged mountains, and narrowing away upwards to where heavy clouds rest upon blue peaks. The wind races through the desolate valley, and finding nothing to resist it but the bridge, whose strong piers stand firmly in the foaming water, it wreaks its vengeance on the storm-clouds, which it collects and scatters at its pleasure, tearing them apart and driving them headlong in front of it, till the valley is flecked with their dark shadows, and with glints of brilliant sunshine between.

We rode through the tiny village of Rudbar, embedded in a wealth of olives, down by the water's edge. Some inhabitant, with a tasteful eye for decoration, had covered the houses with a continuous pattern of red lines and rows of rudely-drawn hands, with the five fingers outstretched, intended to represent the Prophet's hands, and to serve not only as an adornment, but as a charm against evil. We had great difficulty in persuading our baggage-mules to pass by open doors and narrow side streets without satisfying their curiosity as to what lay beyond; they developed all the qualities of ardent explorers, and whenever we were not looking, turned into courtyards and disappeared up slums, Ali Akbar pursuing them with cries and curses, waving his Turkoman lash over his head and dealing blows to right and left. The villagers were gathering in the olive harvest; we shouted to them to throw us some of the fruit, but on experience we came to the conclusion that olives au naturel are not good eating.

Towards mid-day we reached the post-house of Rustemabad, standing half-way up the hillside, and from the platform in front of it we looked across the valley and saw the opposite mountains covered with — forest! Damp, delicious, green forest, trees and trees set thickly over the uneven ground—such a joy to the eye as never was after long months of arid desert, dust and stones! We lunched and changed horses (with some regret, for wisdom had been justified in Ali Akbar, and the Menjil mounts had proved to be excellent, full of spirit and go—a delightful break in the usual monotony of stumbling three-legged brutes), and then we hurried down into the fertile province of Ghilan. Oh, the pleasant forest track all overgrown with moss and maidenhair fern, and the damp, sweet smell of leaves, and the shafts of tempered sunlight between interlacing boughs, and the sound of splashing water! We lifted our eyes only to see the wide Sefid Rud foaming down over his stones, and beyond him more woods, and more and more.

At the bottom of the hill we rested for a few minutes, and drank tea at the caravanserai of the Imam Zadeh Hashem. Here our friendly bridle-path came to an end, and a muddy road lay before us, leading to Resht and the Caspian. We set off with renewed spirits, and traversed the four or five miles between us and our last post-house at a gentle canter. On either side of the road rose a wall of densest vegetation, with here and there a marshy pond covered with rushes, and here and there a tiny clearing, from which the encroaching jungle was with difficulty held back. A luxuriant plant-life covered every stem and every log of wood with moss and ferns, the very huts were half hidden under gourds, which climbed up the walls and laid their fruit and broad leaves across the thatching of the roofs. Charming indeed are the wooden cottages of Ghilan, standing with their backs set into the forest, which has been forced to yield them a foot or two of ground, with verandas supported by columns of rudely-dressed tree-trunks, and with the glow of the firelight (as when we passed that evening) shining through doors and chinks and crevices, while the pleasant smell of wood-smoke rises round them; but the damp climate has set its seal of disease upon the people—they are white and hollow-cheeked, the dark eyes look enormous in the thin faces and glow with the light of fever. They die young, these people, whose meagre bodies are consumed by malaria and shaken by agues.

The post-house of Kudum stands in a small clearing, with ponds round it, the abode of frogs. We found it tolerably comfortable; the swallows which had been nesting in the rafters when we had passed in the spring, and which had disturbed us in the very early hours of the morning with twitterings and flutterings, had fled now, taking their fledged little ones with them; but one of the rooms which was offered to us seemed to belong to someone more important than swallows. His bed was all prepared in it, and on a table were strewn his writing materials, reed pens and inkpots and sheets of paper. We inquired whose was the room of which we had thus summarily entered into possession. 'Oh,' said the people of the post-house indifferently, ' it is only the room of the Naïb.' Now, Naïb means deputy, it is also the title of the Shah's third son, the Commander-in-Chief—who this particular Naïb was we failed to ascertain, but we had visions of a trampling ragged army surrounding our beds late at night, while the Naïbes-Sultan, with the portrait of the Shah blazing in diamonds upon his breast, commanded us in indignant tones to quit the rooms which had been prepared for him, or of waking to find some humbler deputy seated at the table and writing busily with his reed pens complaints of our insolence to his Government. We were undisturbed, however, except by frogs, who croaked unsoothing lullabies in our ears, and by the bells of a caravan of camels which passed at dead of night—an endless train, with silent, ghostly steps, looming out like shadows through the mists, and passing like shadows into the mists again.

Next morning we woke to feel with relief that our ride was over; for the last time we saw our luggage strapped on to the backs of pack-horses, and mounting ourselves into a battered shay, we jolted down the road to the red roofs and the civilization of Resht.

TWO PALACES

MANY, many years have passed since the ingenious Shahrazad beguiled the sleepless hours of the Sultan Shahriyar with her deftly-woven stories, and still for us they are as entrancing, as delightful, as they were for him when they first flowed from her lips. Still those exciting volumes keep generations of English children on wakeful pillows, still they throw the first glamour of mystery and wonder over the unknown East. By the light of our earliest readings we look upon that other world as upon a fairy region full of wild and magical possibilities; imprisoned efreets and obedient djinns, luckless princesses and fortunate fishermen, fall into their appointed places as naturally as policemen and engine-drivers, female orators and members of the Stock Exchange with us; flying carpets await them instead of railway trains, and the one-eyed Kalender seeks a night's shelter as readily in the palace of the three beautiful ladies as he would hie him to the Crown Hotel at home. Yet though one may be prepared in theory for the unexpected, some feeling of bewilderment is excusable when one finds one's self actually in the midst of it, for even in these soberer days the East remembers enough of her former arts as to know that surprise lies at the root of all witchcraft. The supply of bottled magicians seems, indeed, to be exhausted, and the carpets have, for the most part, lost their migratory qualities — travellers must look nowadays to more commonplace modes of progression, but they will be hard put to it from time to time if they do not consent to resign themselves so far to the traditions of their childhood as to seek refuge under a palace roof. It may be that the modern dispensation is as yet incompletely understood, or perhaps civilization marches slowly along Persian roads—at any rate, you will search in vain for the welcoming sign which hangs in English cottage windows, and if the village of mud huts be but a little removed from the track beaten by the feet of post horses, not even the most comfortless lodging will offer itself to you. Fortunately palaces are many in this land where inns are few, and if the hospitality of a king will satisfy you, you may still be tolerably at ease. But luxury will not be yours. The palaces, too, have changed since the fairy-tale days; they are empty now, unfurnished, neglected, the rose-gardens have run wild, the plaster is dropping from the walls, and the Shah himself, when he visits them, is obliged to carry the necessaries of life with him. Take, therefore, your own chicken if you would dine, and your own bed if you have a mind to sleep, and send your servants before you to sweep out the dusty rooms.

It was to the palace of Afcheh, twenty miles to the north-east of Tehran, that we were riding one hot evening. Our road led us across a sun-scorched plain and over a pass, at the top of which we found ourselves looking down on to a long upland valley. A river ran through it, giving life to a belt of trees and corn-fields, and on each side rose the bare mountains which are the Shah's favourite hunting grounds. Down on the river bank stood a tea-house with an inviting veranda, roofed over with green boughs, under which a group of Persians were sitting, listening with inattentive ears to an excited story-teller while he wove some tale of adventure in the sleepy warmth of the twilight. The veranda was screened from the road by clumps of oleanders, whose pink flowers made an exquisite Japanese setting to the cluster of blue-robed peasants. Beyond the tea-house the river was spanned by a bridge, the arches of which were so skilfully fitted into the opposite hill that a carriage—if ever carriage comes—driving down the steep and crooked path must almost inevitably fall headlong into the water below. Night fell as we made our way along the valley; the moon rose, turning the mountain-sides into gleaming sheets of light, filling the gorges with deepest, most mysterious shadow, and after an hour or two of foot-pace riding, we reached the village of Afcheh, our destination.

In the courtyard of the palace preparations for the night were already afoot. In one corner glowed a charcoal brazier, over which the cook was busily concocting a dinner, a table was spread in the middle, and at the further end, protected from the brilliant moonlight by the shadow of a wall, stood a row of camp-beds, for though numberless empty rooms were at our disposal, we had been warned that they were infested by insects, and had chosen the more prudent course of sleeping in the open air. Fortunately, the night was hot and fine, and the court was amply large enough to serve as kitchen, dining-room, and bedroom.

We retired, therefore, to rest, but an Eastern night is not meant for sleep. The animals of the village shared this conviction to the full. The horses, our near neighbours, moved to and fro, and tugged impatiently against their tethering ropes; a traveller riding down the stony streets was saluted by a mad outcry of dogs, who felt it incumbent upon them to keep up a fitful barking long after the sound of his footsteps had died away; and stealthy cats crept round our beds, and considered (not without envy) the softness of our blankets. It was too light for sleep. The moon flooded high heaven, and where the shadow of the wall ended, the intense brightness beat even through closed eyelids. The world was too lovely for sleep. It summoned you forth to watch and to wonder, to listen to the soft rush of mountain streams and the whispering of poplar leaves, to loiter through the vacant palace rooms where the moonbeams fell in patches from the latticed windows, to gaze down the terraced gardens bathed in the deceptive light which seemed to lay everything bare, and yet hid neglect and decay, to strain your eyes towards the shimmering mud roofs on which the villagers snatched a broken rest, turning over with a sigh and a muttered prayer or rising to seek a smoother bed; and yet away towards the dim ranges of mountains that stretched southwards. All the witchery of an Eastern night lay upon Afcheh—surely, if Shahrazad had but once conducted her lord to his open window, she might have spared her fertile imagination many an effort.

In the early hours of the morning the moon set, and darkness fell upon the world, for though the sky was alive with newly revealed stars, their rays were lost in the depths of heaven, and left night to reign on the earth. A little wind shivered through the poplars in the garden, warning us it was time to continue on our way if we would reach the top of the next pass before the heat of day fell upon us, and we drank an early cup of tea in the dark, and waited under the clump of trees that served for stables while the mules were loaded and the horses saddled.

As we waited, suddenly the daystar flashed up over the mountains, a brilliant herald summoning the world to wake. The people on the house-tops lifted their heads, and saw that the night was past. As we rode down the village street they were rising and rolling up their beds, and by the time we reached the valley they were breakfasting on their doorsteps, and the glory of the star had faded in the white dawn. In some meadows watered by the mountain streams a family of nomads had already struck camp, and were starting out on their day's journey; the narrow path over the hills — at best little more than a steep staircase of rock — was blocked by trains of mules laden with coal (black stone, explained our servants); the air rang with the cries of the mule-drivers, and as we rode upwards in cold shadow, the sun struck the mountain-tops, and turned them into solid gold. Day is swift-footed in the East, and man early abroad. Halfway up the pass we paused to look back at our last night's resting-place, but a shoulder of rock hid the palace, and we carried away with us only an impression of the mysterious beauty of its moonlit courts and gardens.

Autumn had come and had almost passed before we found ourselves a second time the guests of the Shah, and under his roof we spent our last two nights in Persia—the one willingly, the other unwillingly.

This other palace stood in the midst of a grove of orange-trees; the waters of the Caspian lapped round its walls, and before its balconies stretched the densely-wooded hills of Ghilan. The Russian steamer which was to take us to Baku (for no Persian flag may float on the inland sea) touched at Enzeli early in the morning to pick up passengers, and we had been advised to pass the night there, so that we might be ready betimes. Accordingly, we had driven through the damp flat country, a tangled mass of vegetation, that lies between Resht and the sea, we had been rowed by half-naked sailors up the long canal and across the lagoons, and in the evening we had reached the peninsula on which the village stands. We were conducted at once to the palace, and, passing down moss-grown garden paths, bordered by zinnias and some belated China roses, we came upon a two-storied house, with deep verandas, and a red-tiled roof rising above the orange-trees. At the top of the staircase we found ourselves in an endless succession of rooms, most of them quite tiny, with windows opening on to the veranda—all unpeopled, all desolate. We chose our suite of apartments, and proceeded to establish ourselves by setting up our beds and dragging a wooden table into our dining-room. Next door to us Ali Akbar had organized his kitchen, and we sat hungrily waiting while he roasted a chicken and heated some boiled rice for our supper. Presently a shadow darkened our doorway, and from the veranda there entered a Persian general dressed in shabby uniform, with some inferior order on his breast, and the badge of the Lion and the Sun fastened into his kolah. He bowed, and politely claimed acquaintance with us, and after a moment of hesitation we recognised in him a fasting official who had come to meet us on our arrival in Persia. The month of Ramazan was then just over, and, in instant expectation of the appearance of the new moon, he had neglected to make a good meal just before dawn. For some reason unknown to us the moon had not been seen that night, and mid-day had found him still compelled to fast. He had sat for full two hours in suffering silence while we crossed the lagoons, but as we paused by the banks of the canal someone had shouted to him that the moon had, in fact, been signalled, and in jubilant haste he had jumped out of our boat, and had rushed away to enjoy his long-deferred breakfast, from which he returned to us smiling, contented, and, I trust, replete. This gentleman it was who now stood upon our palatial threshold; we brought some wooden chairs from one of the numberless untenanted rooms, and invited him and the friend he had with him to enter. They sat down opposite to us and folded their hands, and we sat down, too, and looked at them, and wondered how they expected to be entertained. After an interval of silence we ventured upon a few remarks touching the weather and similar topics, to which they replied with a polite assent that did not seem to contain the promise of many conversational possibilities.

We questioned them as to the condition of Enzeli—what the people did there, how they lived, and, finally, how many inhabitants the peninsula contained. At this our military friend fell into deep thought, so prolonged that we argued from it that he was about to give us the most recent and accurate statistics. At length he looked up with a satisfied air, as though he had succeeded in recalling the exact figures to mind, and replied, ' Kheli !'—' A great many !' No wonder the question had puzzled him. The matter-of-fact European mode of arriving at the size of a village had never before been presented to his Persian brain. How many people? Why, enough to catch fish for him, to make caviare, to sell in the bazaars and tend the orange-gardens—Kheli, therefore, a great many. The interview came to a close when our servant appeared with steaming dishes. Our two guests rose, and, saying they would leave us to the rest and refreshment we must surely need, bowed themselves out.

A curious savour of mingled East and West hung about the little palace. We slept in bare Persian rooms, the loaded orange boughs touched our verandas, and the soft air of the Eastern night rustled through the reed curtains that hung over them; but the brisk, fresh smell of the sea mixed itself with the heavy Oriental atmosphere, beyond the garden walls the moon shone on the broad Caspian, highway to many lands, and the silence of the night was broken by the whistling of steamers, as though Enzeli itself were one of those greater ports on busier seas to which we were speeding.

Speeding? Alas! we had forgotten that we were still in Persia. Next morning the steamer had not come in; we went down to the quay and questioned the officials as to the possible time of its arrival. They, however, shrugged their shoulders in mute surprise at our impatience. How could they know when it might please Allah to send the steamer? We strolled idly through the orange-grove and into a larger pleasure-ground, laid out with turf and empty flower-beds, as though some Elizabethan gardener had designed it—and had left it to be completed by Orientals. The pleasant melancholy of autumn lay upon it all, but of an autumn unlike those to which we were accustomed, for it had brought renewed freshness to the grass, scorched by the summer sun, and a second lease of life to the roses. It was almost with surprise that we noticed the masses of fruit hanging on the green orange boughs which 'never lose their leaves nor ever bid the spring adieu.' In the inner garden stood a tower into whose looking-glass rooms we climbed, and from its balconies searched the Caspian for some sign of our ship. But none was to be seen. In despair we sallied forth into the bazaar, and purchased fish and fowls, honey and dried figs, on which we made an excellent breakfast.

All day long we waited, and how the 'many' inhabitants of Enzeli contrive to pass the time remains a mystery to us. As a watering-place, it is not to be recommended, for the tideless sea leaves all the refuse of the village to rot in the sand; sleep may prove a resource to them, as it did to us, for the greater part of the afternoon and evening; but their lot in the narrow peninsula did not seem to us an enviable one as we hurried through the orange-grove in the dawn, summoned by the whistling of the long-expected boat.

So we steamed away across the Caspian, and the sleepy little place vanished behind the mists that hung over its lagoons and enveloped its guardian mountains—faded and faded from our eyes till the Shah's palace was no longer visible; faded and faded from our minds, and sank back into the mist of vague memories and fugitive sensations.

THE MONTH OF FASTING

OF the powers which come by prayer and fasting, every Mohammedan should have a large share. It is impossible, of course, for the uninitiated to judge how far the inward grace tallies with the outward form, but he can at least bear witness that the forms of the Mohammedan religion are stricter, and that they appear to be more accurately obeyed, than those of the Christian. Religious observances call upon a man with a rougher and a louder voice, and at the same time they are more intimately connected with his everyday life — before the remembrance of the things which are not of this world can have faded from his mind, the muezzin summons him again to turn the eye of faith towards Mecca. The mosques of Constantinople wear a friendly and a homelike air which is absent from Western churches; even those frequented shrines in some small chapel of one of our cathedrals, hung about with pictures and votive offerings, and lighted with wax tapers by pious fingers, do not suggest a more constant devotion than is to be found in the stern and beautiful simplicity of Mohammedan places of worship. At every hour of the day you may see grave men lifting the heavy curtain which hangs across the doorway, and, with their shoes in their hand, treading softly over the carpeted floor, establishing themselves against one of the pillars which support a dome bright with coloured tiles, reading under their breath from the open Koran before them, meditating, perhaps, or praying, if they be of the poorer sort which meditates little, but, however poor they may be, their rags unabashed by glowing carpets and bright-hued tiles. As you pass, slipping over the floor in your large outer shoes, they will look up for a moment, and immediately return to devotions which are too serious to be disturbed by the presence of unbelievers.

To the stranger, religious ceremonies are often enough the one visible expression of a nation's life. In his churches you meet a man on familiar ground, for, prince or beggar, Western or Oriental, all have this in common—that they must pray. We had seen the beggars, we were also to see the Sultan on his way to mosque in Stamboul. He crosses the Golden Horn for this purpose only twice in the year, and even when these appointed times come round, he is so fearful of assassination that he does his best to back out of the disagreeable duty—small wonder, when you think of the examples he has behind him! When he finally decides to venture forth, no one knows until the last moment what route he will take; all the streets and bridges are lined with rows of soldiers, through which, when he comes, his carriage drives swiftly, followed by innumerable carriage-loads of the women of his harem, dressed in pink and blue and green satin, their faces very incompletely concealed by muslin veils—wrappings which are extremely becoming to dark-eyed beauties.

Every Friday Abdul Hamed goes to midday prayers in a small mosque near his palace of Yildiz Kiosk. We stood one sunny morning on the balconies of a house opposite the mosque waiting for his coming; the roads were again lined with soldiers—those tall lean Turks whose grim faces danger and hardship are powerless to disturb—the bands played waltz tunes, the muezzin appeared upon the platform of the minaret, and the Sultan's horses came prancing through the crowds of spectators. Just as he turned into the enclosure of the mosque, a man broke through the crowd and rushed, shouting and waving a roll of paper above his head, towards the carriage window. He pushed his way through two lines of soldiers, with such impetuous force he came, but the third turned him back, still struggling and waving his petition above his head. The waltz tunes drowned his cries, the Sultan disappeared into the mosque, and the petitioner, having been shoved and buffeted from hand to hand, having lost his paper and the better part of his garments in the scuffle, was sent homeward sadly and in rags. When the Sultan came out half an hour later and drove his white horses back through the serried lines of people, the soldiers were again standing with imperturbable faces, and peace had been restored to the Ottoman Empire.

In Constantinople religious observances go far to paralyze the conduct of mundane affairs. Three days of the week are *dies non:* on Friday the Turks are making holiday, Saturday is the Jewish Sabbath, and on Sunday the Christians do no work. Moreover, as far as the Mohammedans are concerned, there is one month of the year when all business is at a standstill. During the twenty-eight days of Ramazan they are ordered by the Prophet to fast from an hour before sunrise until sunset. The Prophet is not always obeyed; the richer classes rarely keep the fast; those whose position does not lift them entirely beyond the pressure of public opinion, soften the harshness of his command by sleeping during the day and carousing during the night — a part of the bazaars, for instance, is not opened until mid-day in Ramazan, at which hour sleepy merchants may be seen spreading out their wares upon the counters with a tribute of many yawns to last night's wakefulness; but the common people still keep to the letter of the law, and to all Ramazan is a good excuse for postponing any disagreeable business.

Such a fast as that enjoined by Mohammed would fill the most ascetic Christian of to-day with indignant horror. Not only is every true believer forbidden to eat during the prescribed hours, but nothing of any kind may pass his lips: he may drink nothing, he may not smoke. These rules, which are to be kept by all except travellers and the sick, fall heavily upon the poorer classes, who alone preserve them faithfully. Porters carrying immense loads up and down the steep streets of Pera and Galata, caïquejis rowing backwards and forwards under the hot sun across the Golden Horn and the swift current of the Bosphorus, owners of small shops standing in narrow, stuffy streets and surrounded by smells which would take the heart out of any man—all these not one drop of water, not one whiff of tobacco, refreshes or comforts during the weary hours of daylight. As the sun sinks lower behind the hill of Stamboul, the tables in front of the coffee-shops are set out with bottles of lemon-water and of syrups, and with rows and rows of water-pipes, and round them cluster groups of men, thirstily awaiting the end of the fast. The moments pass slowly, slowly—even the European grows athirst as he watches the faces about him — the sun still lingers on the edge of the horizon. On a sudden the watchman sees him take his plunge into another hemisphere, and the sunset-gun booms out over the town, shaking minarets and towers as the sound rushes from hill to hill, shaking the patient, silent people into life. At once the smoke of tobacco rises like an incense into the evening air, the narghilehs begin to gurgle merrily, the smoke of cigarettes floats over every group at the street corners, the very hamal pauses under his load as he passes down the hills and lights the little roll of tobacco which he carries all ready in the rags about his waist. Iced water and syrups come later; still later tongues will be loosened over the convivial evening meal; but for the moment what more can a man want than the elusive joy of tobacco-smoke?

From that hour until dawn time passes gaily in Constantinople, and especially in Stamboul, the Turkish quarter. The inhabitants are afoot, the mosques are crowded with worshippers, the coffee-shops are full of men eating, drinking, smoking, and listening to songs and to the tales of story-tellers. The whole city is bright with twinkling lamps; the carved platforms round the minarets, which are like the capitals of pillars supporting the great dome of the sky, are hung about with lights, and, slung on wires between them, sentences from the Koran blaze out in tiny lamps against the blackness of the night. As you look across the Golden Horn the slender towers of the minarets are lost in the darkness, rings of fire hang in mid-air over Stamboul, the word of God flames forth in high heaven, and is reflected back from the waters beneath. Towards morning the lamps fade and burn out, but at dusk the city again decks herself in her jewels, and casts a glittering reflection into her many waters.

On the twenty-fourth night the holy month reaches its culminating point. It is the Night of Predestination; God in heaven lays down His decrees for the coming year, and gives them to His angels to carry to the earth in due season. No good Mohammedan thinks of sleep; the streets are as bright as day, and from every mosque rise the prayers of thousands of worshippers. The great ceremony takes place in the mosque of St. Sophia. Under that vast dome, which the most ancient temples have been ransacked to adorn, until from Heliopolis, from Ephesus, from Athens, and from Baalbec, the dead gods have rendered up their treasures of porphyry and marble—under the dome which was the glory of Christendom is celebrated the festival of the Mohammedan faith. By daylight St. Sophia is still the Christian church, the place of memories. The splendours of Justinian linger in it; the marbles glow with soft colour as though they had caught and held the shadow of that angel's wings who was its architect; the doves which flit through the space of the dome are not less emblems of Christianity than the carved dove of stone over the doorway; the four great painted angels lift their mutilated faces in silent protest against the desecration of the church they guard. Only the bareness, the vast emptiness, which keeps the beauty of St. Sophia unspoilt by flaring altars and tawdry decorations, reminds you that it is a mosque in which you are standing, and the shields hung high up above the capitals, whose twisted golden letters proclaim the names of the Prophet and his companions. Long shafts of dusty sunlight counterchange the darkness, weaving peaceful patterns on the carpeted pavement which was once washed with the blood of fugitives from Turkish scimitars.

But on the Night of Power Christian memories are swept aside, and the stern God of Mohammed fills with His presence the noblest mosque in all the world. As you look down between the pillars of the vast gallery your eyes are blinded by a mist of light—thousands of lamps form a solid roof of brightness between you and the praying people on the floor of the mosque. Gradually the light breaks and disparts, and between the lamps you see the long lines of worshippers below — long, even lines, set all awry across the pavement that the people may turn their eyes not to the East, but further south, where the Ka'bah stands in holy Mecca. From the pulpit the words of the preacher echo round the mosque, and every time that he pronounces the name of God the people fall upon their faces with a great sound, which is like the sound of all nations falling prostrate before their Creator. For a moment the silence of adoration weighs upon the air, then they rise to their feet, and the preacher's voice rolls out again through arches and galleries and domes. 'God is the Light of Heaven and Earth!' say the golden letters overhead. 'He is the Light!' answer the thousands of lamps beneath. 'God is the Light!' reads the preacher. 'God is the Light!' repeats a praying nation, and falls with a sound like thunder, prostrate before His name.

With the Night of Predestination Ramazan is drawing to a close. On the fifth succeeding evening all the Mohammedan world will be agog to catch the first glimpse of the crescent moon, whose rays announce the end of the fast. Woe to true believers if clouds hang over the horizon! The heaven-sent sign alone may set a term to the penance imposed by heavenly decree, and not until the pale herald has ushered in the month of Shawwal may men return to the common comforts of every day.

REQUIESCANT IN PACE

It is a friendly ordering of the world that the episodes of each man's life come to him with so vivid a freshness that his own experience (which is nothing but the experience of all his fellows) might be unique in the history of the race. Providence is but an unskilful strategist, and having contrived one scheme to fill the three-score years and ten, she keeps a man to it, regardless of his disposition and of his desires. Sometimes, indeed, he forces her hand, wresting from her here a little more of power, there a sweeter burst of romance, making her blow a louder peal of warrior trumpets to herald him, and beat a longer roll of drums when he departs; sometimes he outwits her, dying before he has completed the task she set him, or disturbing her calculations by his obstinate vitality. But for the most part he is content to obey, and the familiar story takes its course until death abruptly closes the chapter, and sends the little universe of his deeds to roll unevenly down the centuries, balanced or unbalanced as he left it, with no hand more to modify its course. Familiar and yet never monotonous—though wherever you turn the air is full of memories everywhere the same, though the page of every historian repeats the same tale, though every poet sighs over it, and every human being on the earth lives it over again in his own person. A man will not complain of the want of originality; he is more likely to be cheered when he looks round him and sees his fellows suffering and rejoicing in like manner with himself, when he looks back and sees his predecessors absorbed by the same cares, urged forward by the same hopes. The experience of those who have passed before him along the well-trodden road will not hold him back or turn him aside; to each newcomer the way is new and still to be enjoyed—new and exciting the dangers and the difficulties, new the pleasant sensation of rest by the fountain at mid-day, new and terrible the hunger and the foot-soreness, new, with a grim unexpectedness, the forbidding aspect of that last caravanserai where he lays himself down to sleep out the eternal night. Yes, Death is newest of all and least considered in the counsels of men—Death, who comes silent-footed at all moments, who brushes us with his sleeve as he passes us by, who plucks us warningly by the cloak lest we should forget his presence—he, too, will surprise us at the last.

And if it were not so, small pleasure would be reaped from life. If the past were to stand for ever holding a mirror of the future before his eyes, many a man would refuse to venture forward—it is upon the unknown that he lays his trust—and if the universal presence of death had but once found a lodging in his mind, the whole world would seem to him to be but one vast graveyard, the cheerful fields but a covering for dead men's bones, and the works of their hands but as tombstones under which the dead hands lie.

Yet at times they are good and quiet company, the dead; they will not interrupt your musings, but when they speak, whether they be Jews or Turks or heathens, they will speak in a tongue all can understand. There are even countries where the moving, breathing people are less intelligible, dwell in a world further apart from you, than that silent population under the earth. You may watch the medley of folk hurrying into Stamboul across the Galata Bridge — that causeway between East and West—and the Dervishes washing their feet under the arches of a mosque, and the eager bartering in the bazaars, without one feeling of fellowship with these men and women who look at you askance as you go by; you may pass between long rows of crumbling, closely-latticed houses without venturing to hazard the widest solution of the life within—without even knowing whether there be life at all, so inhospitable they seem, so undomestic. But, once beyond the walls, you have done with distinctions of race. From the high towers of Yedi Kuli on the topmost hill down to the glittering waters of the Golden Horn are scattered countless graves — on the one hand, the triple line of Constantine's city wall, rent and torn, with cracking bastions and dismantled towers, in its hopeless decrepitude still presenting a noble front to all comers, save where the great breach tells of the inrush of the Turkish conquerors Judas-trees drop their purple flowers over the spot where Constantine Palæologus fell, red rose-bushes spring from the crevices, a timid army of lizards garrisons the useless forts. On the other hand, the great city of the dead—acre upon acre of closely-packed graves, regiment upon regiment of headstones, some with a rude turban carved atop, some (and these mark where women lie) unadorned, and all pushed awry by time and storms and the encroaching roots and stems of cypress-trees, all neglected, all desolate. Constantinople, the dying city, is girt about with graves—not more forgotten the names of those that rest there than her own glory on the lips of men. So they speak to you, these dead warriors, dead statesmen, dear dead women, and to the spiritual ear they speak in tragic tones.

The cypresses cast their shadows over this page of Turkish history, springing upwards in black and solemn luxuriance, nourished by dead bodies. The cypress-trees are like mutes, who follow the funeral procession clothed in mourning garments, but with sleek and well-fed faces. They rear their dark heads into the blue sky and beckon to their fellows in Scutari across the Bosphorus.

From the Scutari hill-top the eye is greeted by one of the most enchanting prospects the world has to show—the blue waters of Marmora traversed by greener Bosphorus currents, light mists resting along the foot of the hill-bound coast of Asia, a group of islands floating on the surface of the water, the Golden Horn glimmering away northwards, with the marble walls of the Seraglio stretching a long white finger between it and the sea, Stamboul crowned with minarets and domes. Flocks of gray birds flit aimlessly across the water — the restless souls of women, says Turkish legend — the waves lap round the tower of Leander, the light wind comes whispering down between the exquisite Bosphorus shores, bringing the breath of Russian steppes to shake the plane-leaves in Scutari streets. Constantinople the Magnificent gathers her rags round her, throws over her shoulders her imperial robe of sunshine, and sits in peaceful state with her kingdom of blue waters at her feet. . . . But all around you the dead speak and command your ears. The ground is thick with the graves of men who died fighting, who died of cold and hunger in bleak Crimea; under your feet are great pits filled with unhonoured bones, and the white stones which strew the grass cry aloud the story of struggle and fight into the quiet air. Beyond them the dark canopy of cypresses shadows countless thousands of Turkish graves; the surface of the ground is broken and heaped up as though the dead men had not been content to sleep, but had turned and twisted in their shallow covering of earth, knocking over their tombstones in the effort to force a way out of the cold and the dark into the beautiful world a foot or two above their heads. 'Remember us—remember us!' they cried, as we passed under the cypress-trees. But no one remembered them, and their forgotten sorrows could only send a thrill of vague pity through our hearts.

Not less pitiful in their magnificence are the tombs of the Sultans in Stamboul itself. Here under marble domes, adorned with priceless tiles and hung round with inlaid armour, you may sit upon the ground and tell sad stories of the death of kings, and as you tell of poison and of dagger, of unfaithful wives and treacherous sons, each splendid sarcophagus will serve as illustration to your words. The graves of the dead Sultans are strewn with costly hangings, and set about with railings of mother-of-pearl and precious woods ; plumed and jewelled turbans stand over their heads, their wives lie round them like a body-guard, but gold and pearl and precious stones all serve to blazon forth the tragic histories of those men who lie buried in such mournful state.

With the glitter of this vain pomp before our eyes, we idled on a windy Friday through one of the poorer quarters of the town. A bazaar was being held in Kassim Pasha; women were bargaining over their weekly purchases of dried fruits and grains and household goods ; copper pots lay in shining rows among the coarse crockery and the flowers and cheap luxuries of the poor; the sun shone upon veils and turbans and bronzed faces. It was the hour of mid-day prayer, the little mosque at the end of the street was full to overflowing, the people were kneeling all down the sunny outer steps, rising and falling, bowing their heads upon the stone at the name of God. We paused a moment, and went on round the mosque. In the shadow of a neglected corner behind it, supported on a couple of trestles, lay something swathed in coarse blue linen, with a stick planted into the ground at its head, and surmounted by a discoloured fez. It was the corpse of a man which lay waiting there until the mid-day prayers should be concluded, and his relations could find time for his burial. The wind flapped the corners of his blue cotton coverings to and fro, and shook the worn-out fez, but the dead man waited patiently upon the pleasure of the living—perhaps he knew that he was already forgotten and was content.

In Turkish cities the graves are scattered up and down and anywhere; the stone lattice-work of a saint's tomb breaks the line of houses in every street of Stamboul; wherever there is a little patch of disused ground, there spring a couple of cypresses under which half a dozen tombstones lean awry, and solemn Turkish children play in and out among the graves. We, too, scrambled down the slopes between the half-obliterated mounds, and stood under the shadow of their guardian trees, until the nodding stone turbans wore to us as familiar an aspect as the turbaned heads before the coffee shop in the street.

From time to time, indeed, we remembered the strangeness of this companionship with the generations behind us.

One April afternoon, as we were walking down the steep streets of Trebizond, looking round us with curious eyes, there fell upon our ears a continuous tinkling of bells. We listened: there was no sound of feet, but the bells came nearer and nearer, and at last from one of the narrow streets emerged a camel, and behind him more camels and more, marching on with noiseless padded tread, with impassive Oriental faces and outstretched necks, round which the rows of tiny bells swung backwards and forwards with every step. By their side trudged their drivers, noiselessly, too, in sandalled feet, their faces half hidden by huge caps of long-haired fur, and wearing an expression less human than that of the beasts over which they cracked their whips. 'Look,' said our guide; 'it is a caravan from Tabriz,' and he pushed us back out of the road, for camels have an evil reputation, and are apt to enliven the way by a fretful biting at any person they may happen to encounter. So we stood, without noticing where we had retreated, and watched the long caravan as it passed us with even, measured tread—so slowly that we fell to wondering how many hundred hundred thousand of those deliberate steps had marked the dust and crunched upon the stones across the mountains and valleys and deserts between Trebizond and Tabriz. And though their caravanserai was in sight, the camels never mended their pace, and though they had come so many hundred miles, they did not seem weary with their journey or glad to reach their goal; but as they passed they turned their heads and looked us in the eyes, and we knew that they were thinking that we were only Westerns, and could not understand their placid Oriental ways. When they had passed we glanced down, and found that we were standing upon a grave mound; behind us sprang cypress-trees, and the stone upon which we were leaning bore the dead man's-turban carved upon it. There he lay upon the edge of the great road which he too, perhaps, had trodden from end to end in his day—lay now at rest with the cypresses to shade his head, and the caravans moving ceaseless past him, away and away into the far East. May he rest in peace, the dead man by the living road!

To such charming Turkish sepulchres we looked back as to hallowed resting-places when we had come to know the Persian graveyards. The stretch of dusty stony earth outside the mud walls of the town, the vacant space in the heart of the village where the gravestones were hardly to be distinguished from the natural rockiness of the earth, the home of evil smells, untrodden by living feet, though it lay in the centre of the village life—those shallow graves seemed to us ill-suited to eternal rest. From many of them, indeed, the occupants were to suffer a premature resurrection. After a few months' sleep they would be rudely awakened, wrapped in cloths, and carried on the backs of mules to the holy places. Men who have met these caravans of the dead winding across the desert say that their hearts stood still as that strange and mournful band of wayfarers passed them silently by.

But the pang of sorrow is only for the living. Though we find it hard enough to dissociate sensation from the forms which have once felt like ourselves, the happy dead people are no longer concerned with the fate of the outer vestments they have cast off. They fear no more the heat of the sun, nor the furious winter's rages; the weary journey to Kerbela is nothing to them, nor whether they lie under cypresses, whose silent fingers point to heaven, or under marble domes, or out in the bare desert. Wherever they rest, they rest in peace.

THE CITY OF KING PRUSIAS

AT the foot of the Bithynian Olympus lies a city founded, says tradition, by Cyrus. Philip, the son of Demetrius, gave it to Prusias, King of Bithynia, the friend of Hannibal; Prusias rebuilt it, calling it after himself, and for over two hundred years it was the capital of the Bithynian kingdom. In the first century after Christ it fell into the hands of the Romans; Roman governors took up their abode in Brusa, the younger Pliny described to Trajan the agora, the library, the baths of sulphur, which gave it an honoured place in the civilization of Rome. During the ensuing centuries many men fought and fell for its possession; the cry of battle raged perpetually about its walls. Turks and Christians contended for Brusa, Theodore Lascaris, the Roumanian despot, held it, Orkan ravished it from the Greeks, Timur overwhelmed it with his shepherd warriors from distant Tartary; finally the Turks reconquered it and turned the capital of King Prusias into the capital of the Ottoman Empire.

The soaring minarets, the white domes of mosques and baths, lie amid cypresses and plane-trees at the foot of the mountain. The streams of Olympus, many-fountained like its neighbour Ida, water the town and the surrounding country with such profusion that every inch of ground yields fruit and flowers in tenfold abundance; the hot steam of the sulphur springs diffuses a drowsy warmth through the atmosphere; the city is full of the sound of tinkling fountains and murmuring plane-leaves, and of the voices of black-eyed Turkish children — no wonder if the eagerness of men for its possession drove peace for so many hundred years from its vineyards and olive-groves.

It is said that of the Romans no trace remains. If this be so, the spirit of the Roman builders must have lingered on among Byzantine masons. There is a gateway at the southern side of the town from which part of the stone casing has fallen away, revealing that exquisite brickwork whose secret was known to the Romans only—an entablature of long, narrow bricks, set into arches of complicated pattern, with the sure eye and the even hand that ennoble the commonest materials, and make Roman bricks and plain Roman stonework as beautiful in their way as frieze, or fresco, or marble-casing. Pliny's baths, however, are gone; the present buildings are of Turkish origin.

They lie a little to the east of the town, in fields which vine and olive share with irises and great scarlet poppies. You enter, and find yourself under the dome of a large hall, round the walls of which are railed off compartments where, upon piles of cushions, the bathers rest after the exertion of the bath, smoking a narghileh and drinking a cup of coffee. Beyond this is another and smaller hall, with a fountain of clear cold water in the midst of it, and through various chambers of different temperatures you reach the farthest and hottest of all. The air is thick and heavy with the steam which rises from the blue-tiled basin, where, when the process of washing is over, the Turkish youths swim in the hot water of the sulphur springs, while through the mist the sunlight glimmers down on them from the windows in the dome.

The mosques share the indescribable

charm of Brusa — a charm in which the luxuriant fertility of the land and the accumulated arts of many nations bear an equal part. The tomb of Orkan the Conqueror owes its beauty to the Byzantines, for it lies in the church they reared and dedicated to the prophet Elijah. Before the Green Mosque is a fountain, one of those exquisite fountains of Olympus, shaded by huge plane-trees, and protected by a pointed roof rising on delicate columns, and arches with the Moorish curve in them; and on the mosque itself, the colour of leaves with the sun shining through them is rivalled by the brilliant green of the tiles which encase the dome, and the tracery of laden branches against the sky by the carving round the doorway, until you cannot tell which is the most successful decorator, man or nature. Sultan Mahmud employed Christian workmen in the mosque he built; its architecture wears a curious likeness to that of the West, and the Christian vines and fig-trees are wreathed round the capitals of the Mohammedan shafts. In the big mosque in the centre of the town the builders seem to have recognised that the beauty of curving roofs and the splendour of coloured tiles could go no further—they have called in Heaven to their aid. The entrance, indeed, is vaulted over, the floor is strewn with carpets, and the walls glow with colour; but the central court is open to the sky, and a fountain plashes under the blaze of light and sunshine which falls through the opening. Round the edge of the basin beggars sit washing their feet, grave elders dip their hands and bathe their faces in the cool water; in the columned darkness beyond, bands of Turkish children play at hide-and-seek between the pillars, so noiselessly that they do not disturb the quiet worshippers and the groups of men chatting in undertones, or drown the delicious sound of water and the whispering of the outer airs which fill the building.

Above the town Olympus rears his lofty head: his feet are planted in groves of plane-trees, among the soaring dark spires of cypresses and the white spires of the minarets, beech thickets cover his flanks, and on his shoulders lies a mantle of snow, which narrows and narrows as the summer climbs upwards, but which never entirely disappears.

As we ascended the mountain on our lean ponies, we felt as though we were gradually leaving Turkey behind us, and climbing up into Greece. The snow still lay low enough (for it was in the early summer) to prevent our reaching the summit, yet we could see over the shoulders of the hills the spurs of the beautiful range of Ida, and where the plain of Troy might be on clearer days, with Lake Aphnitis, the furthest boundary of the Troad, gleaming on its edge—'Aphneian Trojans,' says Homer in his catalogue of warriors, 'who inhabit Zeleia at the furthest extremity of Ida, and drink the dark waters of Æsepus.' We could see, too, the long stretch of Marmora and the peninsula of Cyzicus, whose king met with such dire ill-fortune at the hands of Jason, and though this was not that Olympus which was crowned with the halls of Zeus, we comforted ourselves by imagining that Homer may have had the slopes of the Bithynian mountain in the eye of his mind when he wandered singing through the Troad. The beech coppices whispered graceful legends in our ears, the glades, thickset with flowers, seemed to us to be marked with the impress of divine feet — it was the Huntress and her train who had stirred the fritillary bells, Pan's pregnant footing had called the golden crocuses to life, the voices of the nymphs who charmed away Hylas the Argonaut still floated on the air, and through the undergrowth what glimpse was that of flying robe and unloosed shining locks? . . . We rode upward beyond the region of sheltered, flower-strewn glades, beyond the pines, until we came to rough, stony ground, sprinkled with juniper-bushes—and to the very edge of the snow. The mountain-top was all bare and silent; no clash of battle rises now above the plain of Troy; in the blue peaks of Ida, Œnone's cries are hushed; Paris is dead, of Helen's beauty there is nothing but the name; Zeus no longer watches the tide of war from the summit of the Bithynian Olympus, and the nymphs have fled. . . .

The day was nearly over when we descended, the cypresses of Brusa cast long shadows between the white domes—it was the magic moment when the sun, like a second Midas, turns all he touches into gold. The western sky was a sheet of pure gold, the broad plane-leaves hung in golden patterns upon the boughs, the low light lay in a carpet of gold upon the grass, the very air breathed incantations, and on the lowest slope of the mountain we found Ganymede awaiting us. There he sat under a tree by the roadside; he had clothed himself in the semblance of an old Turkish beggar, and hidden his yellow curls beneath a scarlet fez, and the nectar he offered us was only Turkish coffee; but we knew him, in spite of his disguise, when he put one of the tiny cups into our hands, for no coffee brewed by mortal could have tasted so ambrosial or mingled so divine a fragrance with the sweet flowery smell of evening. We sat down on the grass round the primitive brazier—a mere dishful of charcoal set on a shaky iron tripod.

The heavenly cup-bearer was well versed in the arts of coffee-making; he kept half a dozen of his little copper pots a-boiling on the tray of charcoal, which he blew to a red glow round them, and when the coffee frothed up over the edges, he poured it in the nick of time into the cups which we held out to him. The sun flooded our Olympian hall of plane-trees with soft light; we lay in grateful silence upon our couch of grass while the coffee bubbled up over the charcoal fire and frothed steaming into our cups. At length we rose, handed our Ganymede some Turkish coins, at which he must have chuckled in his Greek heart, and rode away in the twilight through the streets of Brusa.

SHOPS AND SHOPKEEPERS

'WE lived together for the space of a month,' related the second of the three ladies of Baghdad to Haroun al Rashid, Ja'far the Wezir, and Mesroor the Executioner, 'after which I begged my husband that he would allow me to go to the bazaar to purchase some stuffs for dress.' She went, accompanied by the inevitable old woman, to the house of a young merchant whose father had recently died, leaving him great wealth. 'He produced all we wanted, and we handed him the money, but he refused to take it, saying : " It is an offer of hospitality for your visit." I said : " If he will not take the money, I will return to him the stuffs." But he would not receive it again, and exclaimed: "By Allah! I will take nothing from you; all this is a present from me for a single kiss, which I will value more than the contents of my whole shop."' The Khalifeh, when the story was concluded — it went on through many and surprising adventures—expressed no astonishment at the young man's generosity. Such an exaggerated view of hospitality seemed to him quite natural on the part of a shopkeeper, nor did he pause to inquire whether the inflammable young man found that the wealth which his father had left him increased with any rapidity through his transactions with pretty ladies.

So reckless a disposition is no longer to be found among Eastern merchants; shopping is now conducted purely on business principles, though it is not without a charm which is absent from Western counters.

Instead of the sleek young man, indistinguishable from his fellows, you have the turbaned Turk, bundled up in multitudinous baggy garments, which he holds round him with one hand, while he takes down his goods with the other; or the keen-featured Persian, from whom you need hope to make no large profit, wrapped in closely-hanging robes, his white linen shirt buttoned neatly across his brown chest; or the specious Armenian in his red fez, cunning and voluble, an easy liar, asking impossible prices for worthless objects, and hoping to ingratiate you by murmuring with a leer that he remembers seeing your face in Spitalfields last time he was there. Shopping with these merchants is not merely the going through of certain forms for the acquisition of necessary commodities—it is an end in itself, an art which combines many social arts, an amusement which will not pall, though many hours be devoted to it, a study in character and national characteristics.

It was in Brusa that we went out to purchase some 'stuffs for dress'—not that we contemplated making for ourselves ten robes each to the value of a thousand golden pieces, like the lady of Baghdad, but that we had heard rumours of certain of the Brusa silks which were suited to less extravagant requirements. It was a hot, steaming afternoon; we hired diminutive donkeys and rode down Brusa streets and under the many domes of the bazaar. The quick, short steps of the donkeys clicked over the cobble stones; we looked round us as they went at the rows and rows of shop-counters, the high vaults which arched away to right and left ward, the courtyards open to the sky, set round with shops, grown over with vines, gleaming with sunshine at the end of some dark narrow passage, the people standing about in leisurely attitudes, and the donkeys, which walked diligently up and down, carrying now a veiled woman sitting astride on her padded saddle, now a turbaned Turk, and now a bale of merchandise. At length we came to the street of the silk merchants, and dismounted before the shop of an old Turk who was sitting cross-legged within.

He rose, and with many polite salaams begged us to enter, and set chairs for us round the low enamelled table. We might have been paying a morning call: we talked —those of us who could speak Turkish—of Sa'di and the musical glasses, we sipped our cups of delicious coffee, we puffed our narghilehs—those of us who could derive any other pleasure from a narghileh than that of a strong taste of charcoal flavoured with painted wood. Presently the subject of silks was broached, and set aside again as unworthy of discussion; after a few more minutes our—host, shall I say?—laid before us a bundle of embroideries, which we examined politely, complimenting him upon his possessions. At length, as if the idea had just struck him, though he knew perfectly well the object of our visit, he pulled a roll of silk from a corner of the shop and laid it before us. We asked tentatively whether he would not permit us to see more, and the business of the afternoon began. The stuffs were certainly charming. There were the usual stripes of silk and cotton, there were muslins woven with tinsel lines, coarse Syrian cottons, and the brocades for which Brusa is famous, mixtures of cotton and silk woven in small patterns something like a Persian pattern, yellow on white, gold on blue, orange on yellow. No doubt we paid more for our purchases than they were worth, but not more than the pleasure of a delightful afternoon spent in the old Turk's company was worth to us.

On our way home we stopped before a confectioner's shop and invited him to let us taste of his preserves. He did not, like the confectioner in the Arabian Nights, prepare for us a delicious dish of pomegranate-seeds, but he gave us Rahat Lakoum, and slices of sugared oranges, and a jelly of rose-leaves (for which cold cream is a good European substitute), and many other delicacies, ending with some round white objects, which I take to have been sugared onions, floating in syrup — after we had tasted them we had small desire to continue our experimental repast.

The bazaars in Constantinople are not so attractive : the crowds jostle you, the shopkeepers, throwing aside Oriental dignity, run after you and catch you by the sleeve, offering to show you Manchester cottons and coarse embroidered muslins. A fragrant savour, indeed, of fried meats and garlic hangs about the eating-shops, on whose counters appetizing mixtures of meat and rice are displayed, and bowls of a white substance like curds, into which a convenient spoon is sticking for the common use of all hungry passers-by, and under the high vaults of the carpet bazaar solemn merchants sit in state among their woven treasures, their silver, and their jewels.

We spent a morning among Persian and Circassian shopmen in Tiflis. There the better part of the bazaar is not roofed over, and the shops open on to a street inches deep in dust or in mud, according to the weather, as is the manner of the streets of Tiflis. They were full of lovely silver ornaments, and especially we noted the heavy silver belts which were hanging in every window and round the waist of every Circassian merchant. We fixed upon one which was being thus informally exhibited round a waist, and, in spite of the many protestations of its wearer, we succeeded in buying it from him. It had belonged to his father, he said, and I think that it was with some reluctance that he pocketed our gold pieces and saw us carrying off his family heirloom.

In Persia the usual order of shopping is reversed: you buy not when you stand in need, but when the merchants choose to come to you. Moreover, the process is very deliberative, and a single bargain may stretch out over months. The counters are the backs of mules, which animals are driven into your garden whenever their owners happen to be passing by. As you sit under the shadow of your plane-trees you become conscious of bowing figures before you, leading laden mules by the bridle; you signify to them that they may spread out their goods, and presently your garden-paths are covered with crisp Persian silks and pieces of minute stitching, with Turkoman tent-hangings, embroideries from Bokhara, and carpets from Yezd and Kerman, and the sunlight flickers down through the plane-leaves into the extemporary shop. There is a personal note about these charming materials which lends them an interest other than that which could be claimed by bright colours and soft textures alone. They speak of individual labour and individual taste. Those tiny squares of Persian work have formed part of a woman's dress—in some andarun, years of a woman's life were spent stitching the close intricate pattern in blended colours from corner to corner; those strips of linen on which the design of red flowers and green leaves is not quite completed, come from the fingers of a girl of Bokhara, who, when she married, threw aside her embroidery-needle and left her fancy-work thus unfinished.

The bargaining begins : you turn over the stuffs with careless fingers—this one is very dirty, that very coarse; you lift a corner of the carpets, and, examining the wrong side with what air of knowledge you can summon to your aid, you mutter that they are only partially silken, after all. Finally you make your offer, which is received with indignant horror on the part of the merchant. He sweeps his wares aside, and draws from the folds of his garments a box of turquoises, which he displays to you with many expressions of admiration, and which you return to him with contemptuous politeness : ' Mal-e shuma !'—' They are your possession !' He packs up his bundles and retires. In a week or two he will return with reduced demands ; you will raise your offer a toman or two, and after a few months of coming and going and of mutual concessions, the disputed carpet will be handed over to you at perhaps half the price that the owner originally asked; or perhaps the merchant will return in triumph and inform you that he has sold it to someone less grasping than you.

Urbane Persian phrases are confusing at first to the brusque European; it was not until we had made several mistakes that we grew accustomed to them.

As we were coming through the garden in the dusk one evening a somewhat ragged stranger accosted us and handed us a long-haired kitten. 'Mal-e shuma!' he said. We were surprised, but since we had been making inquiries for long-haired kittens, we thought that some kind acquaintance had heard of our wants and taken this opportunity of making us a present—presents from casual acquaintances being not uncommon in the East. We thanked the man and passed on with our mewing acquisition. But the Persian did not seem satisfied; he followed us with dogged persistence, and at length the thought struck us that it might not be a gift, after all. We turned and asked:

'What is the cost?'

'Out of your great kindness,' he replied, 'the cost of the cat is three tomans' (about thirty shillings).

'By Allah!' we said, 'in that case it is your possession still;' and we gave the kitten back to him.

When you buy, you might think from the words that pass that you had gained, together with your purchase, a friend for life; and even when you refuse to buy, you veil the terms of your refusal in such a manner that the uninitiated would conclude that you were making a handsome present to your vagrant shopkeeper.

A MURRAY OF THE FIRST CENTURY

THERE are few more curious subjects for observation than the continuity of human life in a given place. Generations of men will go on living on the same spot, though it does not offer them any particular advantages—even though, living there, they must be content with poverty, with insignificance, with a station outside the great swing of the world. 'Some little town by river or sea-shore' is all their universe—not theirs only, but their children's and their children's children's from century to century. You are tempted to believe that these anchored people, who cling like limpets to the rock on which they find themselves, are no more conscious of their own vitality than the limpets their counterparts; rather, it is the town which knows that it exists; with living eyes it watches the coming and going of races, the ebb and flow of the tide of history, trusting in its own immortality, and careless whether Greek or Barbarian, washed up to it on the wave of a folk wandering, fill its walls.

The truth is that man is a stationary animal, and that which seems a backwater of life is the stagnant mid-ocean, after all— that is the first lesson which the East writes in her big wise book, which you may read and read and never reach the last chapter. For the most part, he is unenterprising; he prefers to remain with the evils he knows rather than risk worse fortune in the hope of better, and unless he be driven forth by hunger or by the sword, he will not seek fresh woods and pastures new. It has been said before, and repeated until it should be familiar, that the swift current of Western life is an exception to the general rule, and not the rule itself—said and repeated, and yet when you are brought face to face with tiny towns and remote fishing villages, for whose birth there seems to be no reason but caprice, for whose continuance even caprice can scarcely be alleged, and which may yet boast two thousand years of life, you will stand aghast at such hoar conservative antiquity. Where is progress? Where is the march of civilization? Where the evolution of the race? . . . You have passed beyond the little patch of the globe where these laws bear sway; they are not eternal, still less are they universal, the great mass of mankind is untouched by them, and if you must generalize, you will come nearer the truth in saying that man is stationary than that he is progressive.

On the southern shores of the Black Sea, where the mountains of Anatolia drop their wooded flanks into the water, cluster villages to which the name of progress is unknown; the Greek colonists laid their foundation stones—wanderers they, a seafaring folk of unexampled activity. In those steep valleys and on the open stretches of beach two thousand five hundred years have slipped past almost unnoticed. The Greek names, indeed, have been mutilated by barbarian tongues, and other gods are worshipped on those coasts; the temples of Amisus are buried among brushwood, Mars finds no honour in the island of Aretias, nor does the most adventurous of travellers follow in the steps of Hercules through the mouth of the Acherusian cavern; the slender columns of minarets shoot upwards over the flat white roofs, and the Turk is master in the Bithynian waters. For the rest, what difference? Still from sheltered beaches the rude fishing-boats put forth; still the hard oaks are felled in the mountains and sold in the Byzantium of to-day; still the people till their fields of millet, and gather the wild fruits on the fertile lower slopes; still the harbour of Sinope is filled with the sound of the building of ships, as it was when the Milesian navy anchored behind Cape Syrias. Nay, more—you may journey here with the latest guide-book in one hand and Strabo in the other, and the Murray of the first century will furnish you with more minute information than he of the nineteenth.

For Strabo knew this country well; it was the land of his birth. 'Amaseia, my native place,' lay not far away on the banks of the river Iris, which the Turks call Jeschil Irmak. He praises its fertility, he unfolds its riches, he enumerates every village it contains. He is much occupied, too, with its past history, and to his elaborate researches there is little to be added even to-day, save here and there the story of a Genoese and a Venetian settlement, or of a Byzantine church, and of the final invasion of the Turkish conquerors. He collects much conflicting evidence concerning the origin of divers tribes along the coast—a question which it would puzzle the most learned ethnologist to decide with the materials that lay to Strabo's hand; he notes the boundary of the dominions of Mithridates, and the manner in which the Roman emperors divided the kingdom of Pontus in later times; he sketches the history of Heracleia, the Eregli of to-day, and the birth of the colony of Amastris, which the Turks call Sesamyos, and which was formed by Queen Amastris, niece of Darius and wife of Dionysius the Tyrant, out of four cities—Sesamus, Cytorum (whose green box groves have been famous since the days of Homer), Cromna, and Tieum, the Turkish Tilijos. Above all, he catches at any allusion in the Homeric poems: from these mountains, sings the poet, the warriors marched forth to the defence of Troy; 'From Cromna and Ægialus and the lofty Erythini' they came, they left their country where the wild mules breed, they left the banks of the Sangarius and of that Parthenius stream whose name was tribute to its virgin beauty. I fear the wild mules breed no longer by the river Sakaria, but Ægialus is still to be found under the name of Kara Agatsch, and the lofty Erythini still lift their rocky heads out of the sea.

Some of the places which Strabo mentions were sufficiently unimportant even in his day to have escaped all observation less accurate than his own. Concerning Ak Liman, an anchoring place to the west of Sinope, he quotes a joking proverb: 'He who had nothing to do built a wall about Armene.' Some have fallen from a higher estate, as Sinope itself, which was a naval power of repute in the first century, and the Colchian coast at the eastern end of the Black Sea, which, as he justly remarks, must have been celebrated in the earliest antiquity, as is shown by the story of Jason's voyage thither in search of the Golden Fleece. He explains the legend of the Golden Fleece, by the way, quite in the modern spirit: the torrents of the Caucasus, he says, bring down gold; the Barbarians collect their waters in troughs pierced with holes and lined with the fleeces of sheep, which catch and hold the dust.

Such memories were our travelling companions as we coasted along the wooded shores towards the latter end of the spring. They came rushing in upon us one evening when our ship stopped at a tiny port built at the bottom of a valley sloping down to the water. Intercourse with the outer world is limited to such passing visits of steamers; the inhabitants of the Black Sea villages grow nearly all the necessaries of life in their fertile valleys, and content themselves with a small exchange of wood and dried fruits for cloth and sugar and a few of the luxuries of civilization, amongst which, oddly enough, tombstones are an important item. As we watched the wide Turkish boats, rising high out of the water at stem and stern, which came dancing out towards us over the swell of the waves and poised round us like great sea-birds while the tombstones and the bundles of goods were dropped into them, we fell to wondering, while the evening light faded from land and sea, what the meagre history of Ineboli could be—so remote it seemed, so forgotten — and it presently occurred to us to consult the learned Strabo. There in his book it was duly mentioned: 'Abonteichos, a small city,' 'the modern Ineboli,' added a commentator, and we gazed with different eyes at the small city which was backed by such a long line of experiences.

Next day we reached Samsoun, Strabo's 'Amisus, which Mithridates adorned with temples.' A number of Turks, who were passengers on our ship, disembarked there, for what reason Heaven only knows—Mithridates' pomp has been long since forgotten, and one would think that a man must be hard pressed for occupation before he would seek it in Samsoun. The town lies on sloping ground, rising gently upwards; on the hill behind it we could see the broad road which leads to Diabekir and the people walking in it; the sound of Armenian church bells came to us across the water, and from hour to hour a clock tolled out Turkish time, though no one seemed to heed it. Some Armenian women came on board to examine the ship, and ran up and down the companion ladders, looking at everything with curious eyes and much loud laughter. They were dressed in very bright colours and unveiled, which struck us as indecent in a woman.

Very early on the following morning we woke to find ourselves outside Kerasounde, the Greek Pharnacia — 'a small fortified city,' says Strabo. It was a charming little place, just waking under the misty morning sunshine. Its irregular streets dropped down to the water's edge, and even beyond, for some of the wide-roofed houses were planted out on stakes in the shallow bay. The mountain-side against which it nestled was white with blossoming fruit-trees, and behind it the higher peaks were still white with snow. As for the fortifications, they seem to have disappeared, and, indeed, what foe would turn his arms against Kerasounde?

Towards mid-day we reached Trebizond, and greeted it with almost as much enthusiasm as Xenophon must have displayed when he and his Ten Thousand saw it lying at their feet with the blue sea beyond, and knew that an end was set at last to their weary march. Greek and Roman and Genoese merchant have successively borne sway in Trebizond; fortress walls, churches and monasteries tell of their rule. The Turk has encamped himself now within the fortified limits of the old town, but a large Armenian suburb, half hidden under planetrees, holds to the religion which he displaced.

It happened that on that day the foundations of an Armenian church were being laid, and the Christian town wore a festive air. We watched the ceremony, standing among a crowd of men dressed in their shabby European best, and of women wrapped in white feridgis, with beautiful caps of coins upon their heads. It was not very attractive. A priest was reading prayers before a gaudy picture of the Virgin, a troop of little boys droned Gregorian chants, their discordant voices led by an old man in a fez and blue spectacles, and with no ear for music, who was apparently the choirmaster. Higher up, on the top of the hill overlooking the town, we came upon an interesting and beautiful Byzantine monastery, walled about like a fort—though the walls were in ruins—and with a chapel cut into the solid rock. The chapel walls were covered with frescoes, the half-effaced portraits of saints and of

Greek emperors—those banished Comneni who ruled in Trebizond; a pleasant smell of incense hung about the courtyard, round which were built the cells of the monks —rather dilapidated indeed, but still charming under their roofs of red tiles; blue starch hyacinths lifted their prim heads beneath the apple trees which stood in full flower in the rocky gardens on the hillside, and from the summit of the peaceful walls we could see far inland towards the valleys where the Amazons dwelt, and where, says Strabo, quoting Homer, were the silver mines. Silver is still to be found there, but the Amazons are gone; they might have troubled the good monks in their lodging on the hill-top.

So with regret we returned to our ship, and quitted the cypresses and the plane trees of Trebizond, taking our way 'to Phasis, where ships end their course,' as Strabo quotes (or very near it), thence to pursue our journey by means other than those which the primitive Murray recommends, and through countries which he knew only by hearsay.

TRAVELLING COMPANIONS

ALL the earth is seamed with roads, and all the sea is furrowed with the tracks of ships, and over all the roads and all the waters a continuous stream of people passes up and down—travelling, as they say, for their pleasure. What is it, I wonder, that they go out for to see? Some, it is very certain, are hunting the whole world over for the best hotels; they will mention with enthusiasm their recent journey through Russia, but when you come to question them, you will find that they have nothing to tell except that in Moscow they were really as comfortable as if they had been at home, and even more luxurious, for they had three varieties of game at the table of their host. Some have an eye fixed on the peculiarities of foreign modes of life, that they may gratify their patriotic hearts by condemning them when they differ (as they not infrequently do) from the English customs which they have left, and to which their thoughts turn regretfully; as I have heard the whole French nation summarily dismissed from the pale of civilization because they failed to perceive that boiled potatoes were an essential complement to the roast. To some travelling is merely the traversing of so many hundred miles; no matter whether not an inch of country, not an object of interest, remains in the eye of the mind—they have crossed a continent, they are travellers. These bring back with them only the names of the places they have visited, but are much concerned that the list should be a long one. They will cross over to Scutari that they may conscientiously say they have been in Asia, and traverse India from end to end that they may announce that they have visited all the tombs. They are full of expedients to lighten the hardships of a road whose varied pleasures have no charm for them. They will exhibit with pride their bulky luncheon-baskets, and cast withering glances at that humble flask of yours which has seen so many adventures over the edge of your coat-pocket. 'Ah,' they will say, 'when you have travelled a little you will begin to learn how to make yourself comfortable.' And you will hold your peace, and hug your flask and your adventures the closer to your heart.

All these, and more also, are not travellers in the true sense of the word; they might as well have stayed at home and read a geography-book, or turned over a volume of photographs, and engaged a succession of cooks of different nationalities; but the real travellers, what pleasures are they seeking in fresh lands and strange cities? Reeds shaken in the wind are a picturesque foreground, but scarcely worth a day's journey into the wilderness; men clothed in soft raiment are not often to be met with in hotel or caravanserai, and as for prophets, there are as many at home, maybe, as in other places.

Well, every man carries a different pair of eyes with him, and no two people would answer the question in the same fashion. For myself, I am sometimes tempted to believe that the true pleasure of travel is to be derived from travelling companions. Such curious beings as you fall in with, and in such unexpected places! Although your acquaintance may be short in hours, it is long in experience; and when you part you feel as intimate as if you had shared the same slice of bread-and-butter in your nursery, and the same bottle of claret in your college hall. The vicissitudes of the road have a wonderful talent for bringing out the fine flavour of character. One day may show a man in as many different aspects as it would take ten years of the customary life to exhibit. Moreover, time goes slowly on a ship or in a railway train, and a man is apt to better its pace by relating the incidents of his career to a sympathetic listener. In this manner the doors of palaces and of secret chambers in remote corners of the world fly open to you, and though you may have crossed no more unfamiliar waters than those of the North Sea, you pass through Petersburg and Bokhara, Poland and Algeria, on your way to Antwerp. English people are not so communicative, even abroad, and what they have to tell is of less interest if you are athirst for unknown conditions; their tales lack the charm of those which fall from the lips of men coming, as it were, out of a dream-world, crossing but once the glow of solid reality which lights your own path, and vanishing as suddenly as they came into space. Like packmen, we unfasten our wares, open our little bundle of experiences, spread them out and finger them over : the ship touches at the port, the silks and tinsel are gathered up and strapped upon our backs and carried—God knows where!

The man who carried the most amusing wares we ever examined was a Russian officer, and he spread them out for our inspection as we steamed round the eastern and northern coasts of the Black Sea. He was a magnificent creature, fair-haired, blue-eyed, broad-shouldered, and tall ; he must have stood six feet four in those shining top boots of his. His beard was cut into a point, and his face was like that of some handsome, courteous seventeenth-century nobleman smiling out of a canvas of Vandyke's. He was a mighty hunter, so he told us; he lived with his wife and daughters out in Transcaspia, where he governed a province, and hunted the lions and the wolves (and perhaps the Turkomans also) with packs of dogs and regiments of mounted huntsmen. He was writing a book about Transcaspia; there would be much, he said, of hunt in its pages. He spoke English, and hastened to inform us that every Russian of good family learnt English from his youth up. I trust that the number of his quarterings was in direct proportion to the number of grammatical errors he perpetrated in our tongue, for if so our friend must have been as well connected as he said he was. He told wonderful stories of the wealth and splendour of his family; all the great Slav houses and all their most ancient names seemed to be united in his person. His mother was Princess This, his wife was Princess That, his father had been a governor of such and such a province; he himself, until a few years back, was the most brilliant of the officers in the Czar's guards—indeed, he had only left Petersburg because, with a growing family, he could no longer afford to spend £40,000 a year (or some such sum—I remember it seemed to us enormous). 'And you know,' he added, 'under £40,000 a year you cannot live in Petersburg—not as *I* am accustomed to live.' So he had retired to economize among the lions and the Turkomans until his fortunes should retrieve themselves, which there was every prospect of their doing, since his wife was to inherit one of the largest properties in Russia, and he himself would come into the second largest on the death of his mother. Of that lady he spoke with a gentle sorrow: 'She is very miser,' he would say whenever he alluded to her. 'She send me her blessing, but no pence!' We murmured words of sympathy, but he was not to be comforted—her avarice rankled. 'Ah, yes,' he sighed, when her name came up again in the course of conversation, 'she is very miser!'

It may be that our agreeable companion did not consider himself to be bound by those strict rules of accuracy which tied in a measure our own tongues; his velvets may have been cotton-backed, and his diamonds paste, for all their glitter. We had the opportunity of testing only one of his statements, and I must confess that we were lamentably disappointed. One evening at dinner he was telling us of the prodigies of strength he had accomplished, how he had lifted men with one finger, thrown stupendous weights, and grappled with wild beasts of monstrous size. He even descended into further details. 'In the house of my mother,' he said, 'I took a napkin and bent him twenty times and tore him across!' We were interested, and, to beguile the monotony of the evening, we begged him to perform the same feat on the captain's linen; he acceded, and after dinner we assembled on deck full of expectation. The napkin was produced and folded three or four times; he tore and tore—not a thread gave way! Again he pulled and wrenched until he was red in the face with pulling (and we with shame), and still the napkin was as united as ever. At length we offered some effete excuses—in the house of his mother, even though she was so very miser, the linen was probably of finer quality; no one could be expected to tear one of the ship's napkins, which was as coarse as sackcloth! He accepted the explanation, but nothing is so disconcerting as to be convicted of exaggeration, and though we were heartily sorry for our indiscretion, our acquaintance never again touched those planes of intimacy which it had reached before. Next morning we arrived at Odessa, and parted company with distant bows, nor will he ever, I fear me, send us the promised volume containing some description of Transcaspia and much of hunt.

There is a curious reservation in the communicativeness of a Russian. He will tell you all you wish to know (and more) of himself and of his family, but once touch upon his country or his Government and he is dumb. We noticed this trait in another casual travelling acquaintance, who talked so freely of his own doings, and even of more general topics, such as the novels of Tolstoi, that we were encouraged to question him concerning the condition of the peasantry. 'What of the famine?' we asked. 'Famine!' he said, and a blank expression came over his face.

'I have heard of no famine—there is no famine in Russia!' And yet credible witnesses had informed us that the people were dying by thousands in the southern provinces, not so far removed from Batoum, where our friend occupied a high official position. Doubtless, if we had asked of the Jews, he would have replied with the same imperturbable face—'Jews! I have heard of no Jews in Russia!'

The charm of such friendships lies in their transient character. Before you have time to tire of the new acquaintances they are gone, and in all probability the discussion, which was beginning to grow a little tedious, will never be renewed. You meet them as you meet strangers at a dinner-table, but with less likelihood that the chances of fortune will throw you again together, and less within the trammels of social conventions. Ah, but for those conventions how often might one not sit beside the human being instead of beside the suit of evening clothes! People put on their indistinctive company manners with their indistinctive white shirt-fronts, and only once can I remember to have seen the man pierce through the dress. The transgressor was a Turkish secretary of legation. He was standing gloomily before a supper-table, eyeing the dishes with a hungry glance, when someone came up and asked him why he would not sup. 'Ah,' he sighed, 'ma ceinture! Elle est tellement serrée que je ne puis rien manger!' There was a touch of human nature for you! The suffering Turk said nothing memorable for the rest of the evening, but his own remark brands itself upon the mind, and will not be easily forgotten. I have often wondered at what compromise he and his waistband have arrived during the elapsing years, which must, in spite of all his care, have added certain inches to his circumference.

Not with such fugitive acquaintanceships alone may your fellow-travellers beguile the way : there are many whom you never come to know, and who yet afford a delightful field for observation. In the East a man may travel with his whole family, and yet scarcely interrupt the common flow of every-day life, and by watching them you will learn much concerning Oriental habits which would never otherwise have penetrated through the harem walls. A Turk will arrive on board a ship with half a dozen of his womenkind and as many misshapen bundles, scarcely to be distinguished in form from the beveiled and becloaked ladies themselves. In the course of the next half-hour you will discover that these bundles contain the beds of the family, their food, and all the necessaries of life for the three or four days of the voyage. They will proceed presently to camp out on some portion of the deck roped off for their protection, spreading out their mattresses and their blankets under the open sky, performing what summary toilet they may under their feridgis, eating, sleeping, praying, conversing together, or playing with the pet birds they have brought with them, all in full view of the other passengers, but with as little heed to them as if the rope barrier were really the harem wall it simulates. Meantime, the grave lord of this troop of women paces the deck with dignified tread, and from time to time stops beside his wife and daughters and throws them a word of encouragement.

These family parties may prove of no small inconvenience to other passengers, as once when we were crossing the Sea of Marmora we found the whole of the upper deck cut off from us by an awning and canvas walls, and occupied by chattering women. We remonstrated, and were told that it was unavoidable; the women were great ladies, the family of the Governor of Brousa, with their attendants; they were going to Constantinople, there to celebrate the marriage of one of his daughters with the son of a wealthy pasha. Hence all the laughter and the subdued clatter of tongues, and the air of festive expectation which penetrated through cloaks and veils and canvas walls. But we, who had not the good fortune to be related to pashas, were obliged to content ourselves with the stairs which led on to the deck, on which we seated ourselves with the bad grace of Europeans who feel that they have been cheated of their rights.

Such comparative comfort is enjoyed only by the richer sort; for the poor a sea-voyage is a matter of considerable hardship. They, too, sleep on deck; down on the lower deck they spread their ragged mattresses among ropes and casks and all the miscellaneous detritus of a ship, with the smell and the rattle of the engines in the midst of them, and their rest disturbed by the coming and going of sailors and the bustle of lading and unlading. They cook their own food, for they will not touch that which is prepared by Christian hands, and on chilly nights they seek what shelter they may under the warm funnels. We used to watch these fellow-travellers of ours upon the Caspian boat, setting forth their evening meal as the dusk closed in—it needed little preparation, but they devoured their onions and cheese and coarse sandy cakes of bread with no less relish, and scooped out the pink flesh of their water-melons until nothing but the thinnest paring of rind remained. And as we watched the strange dinner-party of rags and tatters, we fancied that we realized what the feelings of that hasty personage in the Bible must have been after he had gathered in the people from the highways and the byways to partake of his feast, and we congratulated ourselves that we were not called upon to sit as host among them.

Pilgrims from Mecca form a large proportion of the Oriental travellers on the Black Sea. There were two such men on our boat. They were Persians; they wore long Persian robes of dark hues, and on their heads the Persian hat of astrakhan; but you might have guessed their nationality by their faces—the pale, clear-cut Persian faces, with high, narrow foreheads, deep-set eyes and arching brows. They were always together, and held little or no converse with the other passengers, than whom they were clearly of a much higher social status. They stood in the ship's bow gazing eastward, as though they were already looking for the walls of their own Meshed on the far horizon, and perhaps they pondered over the accomplishment of the holy journey, and over the aspect of the sacred places which they, too, had seen at last, but I think their minds were occupied with the prospect of rejoining wife and children and Heimat out there in Meshed, and that was why their silent gaze was turned persistently eastward.

We tried to picture what miseries these people must undergo when storms sweep the crowded deck, and the wind blows through the tattered blankets, and the snow is bedfellow on the hard mattresses; but for us the pleasant summer weather lies for ever on those inland seas, sun and clear starlight bathe coasts beautiful and desolate, sloping down to green water, the playing-ground of porpoises, the evening meals are eaten under the clear skies we knew, and morning breaks fresh and cool through the soft mists to light mysterious lands and wonderful.

THE END.

www.ingramcontent.com/pod-product-compliance
Lightning Source LLC
Chambersburg PA
CBHW030819230426
43667CB00008B/1290